Arthur Ralph Douglas Elliot

The state and the church

Arthur Ralph Douglas Elliot

The state and the church

ISBN/EAN: 9783337261306

Printed in Europe, USA, Canada, Australia, Japan

Cover: Foto ©Lupo / pixelio.de

More available books at **www.hansebooks.com**

The State and The Church

THE ENGLISH CITIZEN:

HIS RIGHTS AND RESPONSIBILITIES.

THE STATE

AND

THE CHURCH

BY THE

HON. ARTHUR ELLIOT, M.P

London
MACMILLAN AND CO.
1882

LONDON: PRINTED BY
SPOTTISWOODE AND CO., NEW-STREET SQUARE
AND PARLIAMENT STREET

PREFACE.

IN the following pages, where it has been necessary to touch at all upon historical topics, I have endeavoured to confine myself to what is generally admitted, rather than to follow the lead of any controversial writer. In Reeves' History of English Law, and in the constitutional histories of Mr. Hallam and Mr. Stubbs will be found, related or referred to, ample matter it is believed to support general statements of an historical character contained in this work.

As regards Ecclesiastical Law, Parish Law, and the more purely legal aspects of the subject included under 'State and Church,' I have had to examine the works of many legal writers. To Sir R. Phillimore's recent work on Ecclesiastical Law are referred those readers who wish to study in detail this branch of the subject.

As regards Scottish history I have in the main relied upon Burton's 'History of Scotland.'

The existing position and circumstances of the Established Churches of Great Britain, favourite subjects with controversial writers, it is not easy to find impartially dealt with outside the contents of Blue-books and Parliamentary returns. It is not the object of this work to accumulate full and precisely accurate statistics, and I have merely made use of such information as I think can be relied on to present a general picture of the two great religious institutions of the country sanctioned and supported by the State.

I must express my thanks to Mr. C. F. Jemmett, B.C.L., of Lincoln's Inn and the Inner Temple, for his great kindness in rendering me valuable assistance in revising the more legal portions of this work.

A. D. E.

May 1882.

CONTENTS.

CHAPTER I.
	PAGE
RISE AND PROGRESS OF THE NATIONAL CHURCH	1

CHAPTER II.
| THE ROYAL SUPREMACY | 19 |

CHAPTER III.
| CLERGY AND LAITY | 23 |

CHAPTER IV.
| CHURCH LAW AND CHURCH COURTS | 40 |

CHAPTER V.
| PAROCHIAL SYSTEM | 55 |

CHAPTER VI.
| THE PRAYER-BOOK AND THIRTY-NINE ARTICLES | 66 |

CHAPTER VII.
| THE REVENUES OF THE CHURCH | 78 |

CHAPTER VIII.

THE CHURCH BUILDING COMMISSION AND THE ECCLESIASTICAL COMMISSIONERS . . . 98

CHAPTER IX.

APPOINTMENT OF DIGNITARIES AND PATRONAGE . 110

CHAPTER X.

'ESTABLISHED' AND 'FREE' CHURCHES . . 124

CHAPTER XI.

THE CHURCH OF SCOTLAND . . . 139

CHAPTER XII.

THE CHURCH OF SCOTLAND (continued) . . 156

STATE AND CHURCH.

CHAPTER I.

RISE AND PROGRESS OF THE NATIONAL CHURCH.

The relationship that exists between State and Church in the United Kingdom at the present day is so peculiar, and differs so much from what we find existing in early times, that it will be necessary, in order to explain it, to take a short retrospect into the religious history of this country. In early times, the mere conception that various religions and Churches could grow up side by side and flourish within the same State would have seemed an impossible one. Throughout Western Christendom, up to the date of the Reformation, there was but one religion and one Church, and for many years after the reformed faith had prevailed over a large portion of Europe, the form of religion decided upon and 'established' in each State became the State religion, all others being either actually persecuted or subjected to civil disabilities of a greater or less degree. When the universality of the prevailing form of Christianity was for ever destroyed by the Reformation, it was found, doubtless, to the surprise of many reformers, that the assertion of the right of private judgment against the claims of authority was as antagonistic to the pretensions of the newer hierarchies as it had shown itself to Papal decrees or Episcopal councils. The transition from the conception of one religion throughout Christendom to that of one religion for each State was a considerable one; but the later transition, which has been less noticed because more quietly accomplished, from a state of things where a 'national' religion was alone professed and tolerated by each nation, to a condition of society where all religions are treated by the State as exactly on the same footing, where, in short, each man's religion is treated by the State as a matter solely within his own cognisance, and with which it will not meddle, is as wide a transition as the former, and the consequences which its complete accomplishment will bring about it is for the future fully to reveal. As the principles of toleration made but slow progress after the triumph of Protestantism, so the later principle of complete religious equality between all religions and all sects follows but slowly upon the removal of civil disabilities. In some countries this principle has already triumphed; and it cannot be doubted that in all countries it is gaining ground. In the United Kingdom at the present day we find in England one form of Protestantism 'established' and closely connected with the State; in Scotland another form of Protestantism also 'established,' though much less closely connected with the State; and in Ireland a system of complete religious equality where each religious body or sect, unfavoured and unprotected by the State, manages its own affairs in the way it thinks best. This state of things would have seemed impossible to our ancestors of pre-Reformation times, when men were as naturally members of the one Church as they were citizens of their own country; and when, as for many centuries was the case, the only persons not of the State religion were the Jews, who, after all, were foreigners as well as infidels. The Church of England was then not merely a part of the nation, but *was* the nation itself, considered in its religious aspect; and to be put by the Church outside its own communion was to forfeit at the same time all the rights of citizenship.

It has been pointed out by several eminent writers that the form of expression, 'the Established Church,' has given rise to a mistaken impression popularly entertained, viz., that at some time or other the law founded or set up the Church; whereas in fact the institution *grew* in the same way that other parts of the Constitution have grown. The Church never was *established*, in the sense in which the Education Department or the Post Office have been established. It is as much part of the original Constitution of the country as the monarchy, which, in point of fact, it long preceded. Its position is, of course, defined and regulated by law, but it does not owe its origin as an institution to any definite act of the legislature or other sovereign authority.

When, in the seventh century, England was still divided among the several Saxon kingdoms of the Heptarchy, Christianity, which had almost disappeared with the overthrow of the Roman power, was again revived by the mission of Augustine. So rapidly did the new religion spread among the people, that by the middle of the eighth century it had been accepted in each of the kingdoms and the whole country had been divided into dioceses, which were grouped into the two provinces of Canterbury and York. The monks who had accompanied Augustine, and their successors, spreading by degrees further and further from their central establishments, carried their religion into the remoter districts. Yet the nation, or rather the nations, were converted, so to speak, from above; the kings and rulers being gained first, and their subjects following.[1] 'The State,' in fact, adopted the new religion, whose ecclesiastical system thus became founded on a political basis. Dioceses are said, in the first instance, to have been commensurate with kingdoms, and parishes with townships. By the end of the eighth century ecclesiastical conclaves had been held, and the payment of tithe had been ordered by a legatine council with the sanction and approval of the King.

The northern part of England, however, owed its Christianity rather to the Scottish monks from Iona than to the Roman followers of Augustine. The Scottish religious practices, like those surviving among the British in Wales, were of the Greek rather than of the Roman type. In the much-disputed question of the celebration of Easter, as well as in the peculiar form of monkish tonsure, the Celtic Christians followed the Eastern

---

[1] See the interesting account given in Milman's *Latin Christianity*, bk. 4, cap. iii.; of the conversions of the kings of Kent and of Northumberland. And Mr. G. Harwood's *Disestablishment*.

Church. As time went on the Roman practices everywhere ultimately prevailed, and it would hardly have been necessary to refer at all to Celtic Christianity were it not that a party in the Church of England at the present day attaches importance to whatever tends to show the early independence of the English Church as regards Roman authority and its closer connection with Greek Christianity.

Down to the time of the Norman Conquest the Church of England remained peculiarly a national church, honouring its own saints, observing its own festivals, and conducting its services in the national tongue. Little interfered with by the Churches of the Continent, it developed itself spontaneously with the growth of the nation; and, after the Saxon rule was ended by the invasion of William the Conqueror, the Church for long kept alive the recollection of popular rights and liberties, and as a body showed in the prolonged resistance to Papal claims that its national character had not been lost.

The Papal influence, nevertheless, from the Conquest to the Reformation, supported by the monasteries and with many of the principal ecclesiastics devoted to its service, endeavoured steadily to extend itself at the expense of the liberties of the local Church as well as of the national independence. Throughout Europe the tendency was more and more to centralize ecclesiastical authority and power at Rome.

With the reign of the Conqueror came a sharp division between the civil and ecclesiastical jurisdictions. Probably in Saxon times there had been very little distinction recognised between these jurisdictions; but now we find, by an ordinance of the Conqueror, that the bishops are forbidden to hold pleas *de legibus episcopalibus* in the Hundred Court, or to submit to the judgment of secular persons any cause relating to the cure of souls. Henceforth, whoever had offended against the Episcopal laws was to answer the cause and do what was right towards God and the bishop, *not* according to the law used in the Hundred, but *according to the Canons and the Episcopal law*, and any sentence of excommunication which the bishop might pass was to receive the full support of the royal authority. The separation of jurisdiction thus begun, tended to become wider and wider. Pontifical decrees and Church law having for their object to enlarge the authority of the ecclesiastical tribunals succeeded, to a great extent, in establishing the exemption of the clergy from the common law and the ordinary law-courts of the country. Not content with this, the spiritual courts claimed exclusive control over many of the most important matters of civil life. It was their province to decide upon all questions of wills, of legitimacy and of marriage, and a claim was even set up to judge of contracts, on the ground that breach of faith was a spiritual offence of which the spiritual court should have cognisance. To limit the encroachments of the clergy the kings in early times, by their constitutions or their charters, endeavoured to define the limits of ecclesiastical authority, and in later days many Acts of Parliament were passed with the same object. When it was open to anyone arraigned or convicted of crime before a lay tribunal to claim exemption from its jurisdiction and be handed over to the ordinary (*i.e.*, the bishop), 'to claim his clergy,' as it was called, the sole test being his capacity to read, 'quod legit ut clericus ideo tradatur ordinario,' we may imagine to what a degree the authority of the King's courts had been reduced.

And there were many other points in which, even in the most orthodox times, the State and the ecclesiastical authority differed. It was not only that the nation did not like to see its common law, with its marked feature of trial by jury, continually limited by the encroachments of a rival and foreign system, whose ultimate court of appeal was outside the kingdom. A dislike was also naturally felt to the system of Papal exactions, and of Papal patronage, to the filling of dignified and lucrative positions in the National Church with foreign ecclesiastics, and to the assertion of Papal authority, assented to by an English king, that his crown was held under the feudal supremacy of the Bishop of Rome, for which tribute was justly due. These feelings, whether of a practical or sentimental nature, prove that, however much in one sense Church and State may in orthodox days have been composed of the same individuals, the rivalry between those who leaned to ecclesiasticism and those who leaned to nationalism must necessarily have been a keen one.

The first chapter of Magna Charta stipulates that the Church of England (Anglicana Ecclesia) shall be free and have her whole rights and liberties inviolable; one of the most valued of which was the right of the Chapters and religious houses to elect their bishops and abbots, instead of having a choice forced upon them by the King or the Pope. Again, the jealousy of foreign interference is shown in the preamble to a statute of Edward I., which recites that the Church of England was founded by the kings and nobles of the realm for their instruction and that of the people; that sees and rents had been appropriated by the said founders to the prelates and other beneficed persons, that thence resulted the right of collation and presentation claimed by the King and his nobles, that the higher order of such clergy constituted a considerable part of the King's great council to advise him in national affairs, and that consequently it was a grievance that the Bishop of Rome should, invading the rights of others, grant dignities to cardinals and other men, who were aliens, as if he were the patron; and, therefore, it was enacted that all elections to Church preferments that were elective should be free as in time past.

But not only did the clergy possess its separate judicatories, in which was administered its own system of law; it constituted also a separate order in the State, exempt from the taxation of Parliament, claiming to legislate for itself in the convocations of the provinces of Canterbury and York, and regularly summoned along with the Parliament to aid the Crown with its supplies. In ecclesiastical affairs down to the Reformation the supreme legislative authority was disputed between *the State*, *i.e.*, the King and Parliament, *the Pope*, whose legate and representative in England was usually the Archbishop of Canterbury, and *the Church of England*, speaking through its constituted authorities in its provincial or national assemblies. Till the fall of the mitred abbots under Henry VIII., the ecclesiastical element in the House of Lords considerably outnumbered the temporal Peers. The clergy, moreover, were possessed of immense wealth. Though not endowed territorially by the law, which indeed had often endeavoured to check the acquisitiveness of the Church, the monasteries and ecclesiastical corporations had become possessed of enormous estates through the piety of donors and testators, and through the rule that property once devoted to religious uses could not again, without sacrilege, be applied to secular purposes. Nevertheless, under Henry V. many of the monasteries of alien monks had been suppressed, and their lands annexed to the Crown, and, again, as a consequence of the visitations of Cardinal Wolsey, corrupt establishments had been destroyed and their wealth applied to the purposes of public education. It is calculated that these religious houses at one time owned nearly one-fifth of all the land of the kingdom; and in Scotland, a much poorer country, it is probable that they were, proportionately, better endowed, thanks in great measure to the piety of the canonised King David, whose magnificent foundations have made him known to posterity as a 'sair saint for the Crown.'

The English dispute with Rome did not arise out of any strictly religious difference between the Pope and the King. The latter had earned from the former the title of Defender of the Faith, for the vigorous orthodoxy with which he had attempted to confute the doctrines of Luther; and, however anxious Henry proved himself to diminish the Papal authority in England, and however the necessity of his struggle with Rome may have forced him to side with the Protestant party, he always remained attached to those Catholic doctrines which specially roused the hostility of the Reformers. In short, his policy was to overthrow the Papal power, not to attack the doctrines of the Romish Church, and whatever policy he pursued, he found his Parliament ready to give him its support. Appeals to Rome were abolished by a statute, which declares, 'in maintenance of the ancient law of the land,' that all questions of divorce, matrimony, tithes, &c., should be *finally* determined within the King's jurisdiction, and not elsewhere, in spite of any excommunications or interdicts to the contrary. And by subsequent Acts it was provided that for the future appeals should be brought from all the ordinary ecclesiastical courts in England and Wales to the King in Chancery, and that upon every such appeal a commission should be directed to such persons as should be named by the King (afterwards known as the Court of Delegates), that all existing canons, constitutions, and ordinances not repugnant to the laws and customs of the realm or to the King's prerogative should continue in force as before, that bishops should be appointed by royal letters patent,[1] and that the King should be taken to be 'the only supreme head on earth of the Church of England, called Ecclesia Anglicana, and should have all authority thereto annexed to reform and correct all errors, heresies, and abuses which may be amended by any spiritual jurisdiction whatsoever.' And this, at a time when Parliament was imposing the punishment of death on any one denying the doctrine of the Real Presence, and making it felony to preach in favour of the marriage of priests

[1] 31 Henry VIII. c. 9.

or against the celebration of the mass. The Royal supremacy was thus to be substituted for the Papal supremacy, but the Church was otherwise to be left a complete organisation, with its own laws and its own courts, independent of all authority but the King's. Henry VIII. had made this very plain even before the actual rupture with Rome; for when some of the clergy had declared that an Act of Parliament withdrawing 'benefit of clergy' from murderers and robbers was contrary to the law of God and to the liberties of the Church, he refused to delay judgment till the matter had been referred to the Pope. 'By the order and sufferance of God we are King of England, and the Kings of England who have gone before us never had any superior but God alone, and therefore know that we will maintain the right of our crown and temporal jurisdiction, as well in this point as in others, in as ample a manner as our predecessors have done before us. And as to your decrees, we are well assured that you yourselves of the Spiritualty act in contradiction to the words of many of them, as has been shown you by some of our spiritual counsel on this occasion. And besides you interpret your decrees at your pleasure; therefore we will not conform to your will and pleasure more than our progenitors have.' The King was evidently of opinion

> That men can construe things after their fashion
> Clean from the purpose of the things themselves;[1]

and whether right or wrong in this belief his eminently Tudor speech is a good illustration of the spirit which caused and maintained the rupture with the See of Rome; but whether the motives of Henry, Edward,

[1] *Julius Cæsar.*

and Elizabeth were chiefly religious or chiefly political, the course that was pursued by them and their Parliaments, in breaking up the monasteries, in expelling the mitred abbots from the House of Lords, and in exalting and enforcing the royal supremacy in all ecclesiastical matters of importance, gave a blow to the power of the clergy in the State, and to the authority of that order even in things ecclesiastical, which has reduced it to a very different position to that it formerly held. In England, more probably than elsewhere, the Reformation was under the guidance of temporal and political rulers, rather than of religious enthusiasts, and the character thus originally impressed on the English Protestant Church—and its habit of looking to political as much as to purely ecclesiastical or religious considerations—have been very marked throughout its later history. It was in the reign of Elizabeth that the Church of England finally assumed its present shape. By that time the Articles of Religion, and even the Prayer Book, had substantially assumed their present form, and had received the sanction of Parliament. Yet though Elizabeth's acts of supremacy, of uniformity, and of assurance, secured the Protestant establishment, it was due to her personal predilections for Roman ritual and external ceremonial prevailing over the wishes of her subjects, and even over those of her most distinguished bishops, that those observances were retained which led to the great Nonconformist separation from the Anglican establishment. The legislation of her reign, like that of her brother and father, shows clearly that it was then held to be the unquestioned duty of the ruling authority of the nation to impose and uphold one form of religion. *All* ministers were to use the Book of Common Prayer; *all* persons were to resort on Sundays to the parish churches; and neither Act of Parliament, nor determination of any religious or ecclesiastical cause under its authority, was to be adjudged heretical or schismatical, in spite of any ecclesiastical decree or canon to the contrary. Jesuits and seminary priests were expelled the kingdom, and it was even made high treason to convert anyone to the Roman religion; but this was later in the Queen's reign, when the Protestantism of the Parliament, which was much more decided than that of the sovereign, had got fuller sway. Extreme Churchmen of different religious communities were equally zealous in claiming the assistance of the State, and in repudiating its authority. At the beginning of Elizabeth's reign Archbishop Parker sent for Mr. Wentworth, a distinguished Puritan member of Parliament, to ask him why the House of Commons had put out of the Prayer Book the 'articles for the homilies, consecration of bishops and such like.' 'Surely, Sir,' said I, 'because we were so occupied in other matters that we had no time to examine them, how they agreed with the word of God!' 'What!' said he, 'surely you mistake the matter: you will refer yourselves solely to us therein!' 'No! by the faith I bear to God,' said I, 'we will pass nothing before we understand what it is; for that were but to make you Popes; make you Popes who list,' said I, 'for we will make you none. And sure, Mr. Speaker, the speech seemed to me to be a Pope-like speech, and I fear lest our bishops do attribute this of the Pope's Canons unto themselves; " Papa non potest errare.'"[1] That this pretension of the Church to dictate true religion to the nation, and then to have the support of the arm of the State, was as strongly put forward by the extreme Presbyterians as by the Archbishop of Canterbury is evident from the declaration made by their leader Cartwright that it was the duty of the Sovereign 'to protect and defend the councils of his clergy, to keep the peace, to see their decrees executed, and to punish the contemners of them, but to exercise no spiritual jurisdiction. It must be remembered that civil magistrates must govern the Church according to the rules of God prescribed in His word; and that, as they are nurses, so they be servants to the Church; and as they rule in the Church, so they must remember to submit themselves unto the Church, to submit their sceptres, to throw down their crowns before the Church—yea, as the Prophet speaketh, to lick the dust off the feet of the Church.' Fortunately, ecclesiastical pretensions of this sort, from whatever side they have come, have never found any permanent favour with the English people. Neither was the royal claim to personal supremacy as evidenced above by King Henry's words likely to remain unquestioned, when monarchs of less ascendency than the Tudors found themselves at issue with subjects who had become more alive to their rights and liberties than those who had gone before them. Towards the end of Elizabeth's reign, she had ordered her Parliament not to meddle with religious matters till they had been considered by those better able to understand them; but after her death that

---

[1] D'Ewes's *Parliamentary History*, quoted in Hallam's *History of England*.

change began which has gradually transformed the personal action of the monarch into what we should now call the constitutional action of the crown: in which the action of the crown represents the highest expression of the will of the State.

The policy of the Tudor sovereigns and the claims of extreme Episcopalians and of extreme Presbyterians have been here dwelt upon, because they appear to illustrate conflicting theories of Church government, with which, in a slightly modified form, we still have to deal. There are still among us Churchmen of different religious communities who would wish the State to be no more than their servant, and who consider themselves entitled to treat with contempt the law of the land, because it does not conform with what they may choose to consider the law of their Church. There is, on the other hand, a predominant sentiment in the public mind that the nation at large is concerned in the conduct and position of the Established Church, and that the final authority in things ecclesiastical as well as temporal must be the will of the nation as expressed in the laws which it has made, or in the constitutional action of the Crown.

Since the times of which we have been writing, the relationship of the Church towards the State has undergone considerable change, yet this is not so much in consequence of changes introduced into the constitution of the Church of England itself, which, indeed, remains much as it was, as of the very different position in which those who are not members of that Church now find themselves. Nonconformists and Dissenters having early succeeded in getting their religion tolerated, have at last acquired all the civil rights enjoyed by orthodox Churchmen. We shall see later in this work in what the 'Establishment of the Church' now consists, and how it differs from the purely voluntary system of Church government which has sprung up around it. The National Church, in the old sense, of the whole nation considered in its religious aspect, it has, of course, now no claim to be; since a very large portion of the commuuity looks for its religion to other Communions, and does so without being visited by any penalty or disqualification by the State; but it remains, nevertheless, so far the National Church that the nation, through its Parliament and through its ordinary courts of law, is the supreme power which regulates it, that its ministrations, religious services, and churches are open to all citizens alike, and that a large portion of its wealth and support is derived not from voluntary sources, but from the provisions anciently made to provide for the old State religion. It will suffice for the present to point out that the principal characteristics of the connection between Church and State in England are:—

1. The royal supremacy.

2. The subordination of the Church to Parliamentary control.

3. The presence of the archbishops and bishops in the House of Lords.

4. The national endowment of the Church.

5. The accessibility of the Church to all who may wish to avail themselves of its ministrations.

The Establishment is further brought into relationship with external influence by 'Church patronage,' as will be afterwards explained.

To summarise shortly what has been said, we find in the earliest times a Church very national in character, and of thoroughly spontaneous growth, which, from the Norman Conquest down to the Reformation, it had been the object of the Popes, supported by the monkish orders and by some of the higher ecclesiastical dignitaries, to render subject to the See of Rome. Hence the struggle in English, as in Continental history, as to investitures, rights of patronage, papal exactions, and the like. We find the clergy constituting a separate order in the State, exempt from Parliamentary taxation, and to a great extent from the control of the ordinary courts of law; whilst from their own ecclesiastical courts the ultimate appeal lay to the Pope. Thus, long before there was any serious question of a change taking place in the *religion* of the country, we find a fierce and prolonged rivalry between the State and the ecclesiastical organisation which centred in Rome. Henry VIII. substituted his own for the Papal supremacy, and, the religious Protestantism of his successor being in favour with the growing sympathies of the country, the change which Henry had intended to create in the relationship of the English Church towards Rome developed itself under those who came after him into an absolute rupture between the Roman Catholic religion and that of the English nation. With the final rupture with Rome and the reformation of religion came the alienation of much Church property, the suppression of the monastic orders, and, practically speaking, the fall of the clergy as one of the orders of the State. For some time after the complete overthrow of Roman authority we find it the accepted theory of the State that it should prescribe and enforce what it deemed the true religion; while religious leaders, such as Laud in England and the Covenanters in Scotland, differing as to which was the true religion, agreed that the State should use its authority to enforce the doctrines and system which 'the Church' should prescribe. This extreme Church view, however, did not prove very acceptable to the English people; and we find a tendency steadily increasing, from the first manifestation of Protestant Nonconformity down to the present time, to diminish and ultimately to abolish all civil distinctions between those of different religious persuasions. Hence the spread of the principle of toleration and the growth of that of religious equality.

CHAPTER II.

THE ROYAL SUPREMACY.

THE supremacy of the Crown of England in matters ecclesiastical has been claimed by Lord Chief Justice Hale as being part of the old common law,[1] and it was certainly recognised by statute at a very early date. But in what sense this 'supremacy' was understood when the Papacy was undoubtedly in fact the spiritual head of the Church, it is not very easy to discover. At the present day it is by virtue of her supremacy that the sovereign convenes, regulates, and dissolves all ecclesiastical convocations, which without her summons could not lawfully assemble for business. It is by virtue of her prerogative that she nominates the higher dignitaries of the Church, and it is due to her supremacy that a final appeal lies from all the ecclesiastical courts to the Queen in Council. The actual expression of 'Supreme Head of the Church and clergy of England' appears first in the petition of Convocation to King Henry VIII. to relieve them from the penalties to which they were exposed. The petition was followed by the statute called the Act of Submission, which, having recited this recognition of

[1] Hale's *History of the Common Law*. See also Cawdrey's Case, 5 Coke, p. 75.

the royal supremacy by the whole clergy in Convocation, in order to make assurance doubly sure, enacted that the King should be reputed the 'only supreme head in earth of the Church of England, and should have annexed to the imperial crown of this realm as well the style and title thereof, as all jurisdictions, authorities, and commodities to the said dignity of the supreme head of the Church appertaining.'[1]

Convocation, however, had only in fact recognised 'the Headship, so far as was permitted by the law of Christ, a qualification not taken any notice of by the Act of Parliament. The sense in which the supremacy is now understood is further developed by the Thirty-seventh Article of Religion (which is binding by virtue of the authority both of Convocation and of Parliament), where it is explained that though the sovereign is recognised as the ruler of all ecclesiastical estates and degrees, she is not to be supposed to have had given to her any spiritual authority to perform the duties of the Christian ministry. Again, by the Canons[2] and constitutions of the Church of England the recognition of the supremacy is very full, as the 'King's power within his realms' is declared to be 'the highest power under God, to whom all men do by God's laws owe most loyalty and obedience, afore and above all other powers and potentates in the

---

[1] This Act was repealed under Mary, but the Royal supremacy was restored in the first year of Elizabeth.

[2] See Canons I. and II. 1603. These Canons published by the royal authority somewhat alarmed the House of Commons, which resolved that the Kings of England had no power to alter religion, or to make any laws concerning it, otherwise than in temporal matters, that is by consent of Parliament.

earth.' And the next Canon, in order to elucidate the nature of the royal authority in causes ecclesiastical, explains that it is the same that ' the godly kings had amongst the Jews, and the Christian emperors of the primitive Church.' And should any one be so bold as to impeach the royal authority, he is to be excommunicated *ipso facto,* and not to be restored until he has repented and revoked 'those his wicked errors.' It need scarcely be stated that any action of the Crown, in the exercise of its prerogatives, whether in ecclesiastical matters or in civil, whether in judicial or administrative business, must be constitutional; that is, it must be taken upon the advice of a responsible Minister, or on that of an established tribunal. This relation of the Crown to the Established Church is peculiar to England. In Scotland the Church has always guarded itself against any admission of a temporal 'Headship,' and in Ireland the royal authority withdrew from all interference in ecclesiastical matters when the Establishment was put an end to in 1869. At the union in 1801 it was enacted that the Churches of England and Ireland were for ever to form one Protestant Episcopalian Church, and this was to be a fundamental part of the union between the two countries; but this legislative attempt to bind futurity of course was not allowed to hamper the nation, a couple of generations afterwards, in pursuing a policy which it considered both just and expedient. We need not say more here with reference to the supremacy, the operation of which will appear incidentally in later portions of this work; but it should be noticed that it is due in great measure to this connection between the Church and the

Head of the State that the voice of statesmanship has been so often heard in England above the clamour of ecclesiastics. It has, in fact, given an importance to the lay element in the nation, to which an unchecked episcopalian system would have denied a hearing.

Such being the relation between the Church and the Sovereign, it is natural that some security for the religion of the latter should be taken by the law. Accordingly it is provided that the Sovereign must be 'Protestant,' and that his entering the Roman Communion or marrying a Papist is to forfeit the Crown and absolve his subjects from their allegiance. Every Sovereign ' on coming to the possession of the Crown shall join in communion with the Church of England as by law established,'[1] and in the Coronation Service, which must be performed by an archbishop or a bishop of the Established Church, the Sovereign undertakes ' to maintain the laws of God, the true profession of the Gospel, and the Protestant reformed religion established by law,' and to 'preserve to the bishops and clergy of the realm, and to the churches committed to their charge, all such rights and privileges as by law do or shall appertain unto them.'[2]

[1] 12 & 13 William III., cap. 2, section 3.
[2] 1 William & Mary, cap. 6. See also the Act of Union of 1706.

CHAPTER III.

CLERGY AND LAITY.

The Church consists of clergy and laity, though the word has been too often employed as if 'the Church' was synonymous with 'the clergy.' It was said by one Dean of Westminster, and the saying has been quoted with approbation by another, 'that though it might be thought an absurdity to call the large body of the laity "the Church," to the exclusion of the clergy, it is a far greater absurdity to call the small body of the clergy "the Church," to the exclusion of the laity.'

The clergy, then, are those members of the Church who are specially set aside by its own rules and by the law of the land to perform its services, to conduct its ministrations, and to teach its doctrines. Their privileges and their disabilities, their duties and their rights, in short, their whole status in the community at large, are part of the general law of the kingdom.

That larger portion of the Church called the laity is much less clearly defined. Originally all were members of the Church, for, as we have seen, the State for long refused to recognise any diversity from its own religion. It is still true that all subjects of the Crown are entitled to the benefit of the services of the established clergy;

all alike may enter the national churches, and use the national churchyards. No one can be debarred but by himself from participating in the advantages offered by the Establishment. Still, at the present day, we have to recognise the fact that the State religion is but one among many; that its services are rejected and its doctrines disputed by other Churches, and thus, that though all citizens have the legal right to avail themselves of the religious ministrations provided by the State, it is a right which only a portion of the subjects of the Crown are in a position, as a matter of fact, to make use of. What constitutes lay-membership of the Church of England it is not easy to say. The expression is not one to which any legal definition has been given. As regards creed, the late Dean of Westminster tells us 'that the only test, in fact, of membership in the English Church is the Apostles' Creed.' Some, on the other hand, might prefer to limit true membership to communicants, or even to such as comply with the injunction of the 21st Canon, as to receiving the Communion at Easter, and on two other occasions in each year. For practical purposes the meaning generally attached to the expression seems the best, viz. that all are laymen of the Church of England who signify a general assent to its doctrines and practices by customarily using its ministrations.[1]

Thus any calculations as to the numbers of the laity must be necessarily of a very vague character, and may very likely even mislead; for, as has been already stated, it is not to any limited body, *but to all who may require it,*

---

[1] See Blunt's *Book of Church Law.*

that an Established Church offers its assistance and opens its doors. The number of church-goers may be got at (very roughly) by taking account of the number of churches, and of sittings provided. In 1876 the Church of England could reckon about 16,000 churches, and this has been calculated as providing, in all probability, nearly 6,000,000 sittings; while in the same year it was estimated that there was one church to every 1,500 of the population.

The other portion of the Church, namely, the clergy, it is much more easy to number.

In 1876 a Select Committee of the House of Commons was appointed, to which the Public Worship Regulation Bill was referred, and a statement of the numbers of the clergy taken from the Clergy List was laid before it. This showed their total number of all grades to amount to nearly 25,000. It is worthy of notice that, in comparison with the enormous growth of population in recent years, there has been nothing like a proportionate increase in the numbers of the clergy. In 1811, when the population of England and Wales did not much exceed 10,000,000, the number of the active clergy was about 16,000, while in 1871, with a population considerably over 22,000,000, the same class did not number much over 19,000.

The clergy are those who have been admitted into holy orders, of which the Church of England recognises three kinds, viz. those of bishops, priests, and deacons; and no one is permitted to take upon himself the office of public preaching or of exercising the ministerial functions until he has first been 'lawfully called,' and authorised to the performance of the duty. The ministerial capacity can be bestowed only by episcopal authority, and by the imposition of hands; it being the belief of the Church of England that the division of the ministry into three orders, and this method of bestowing spiritual authority to exercise ministerial functions, were prescribed by the Apostles at the very foundation of the Christian Church.[1] Yet though this view is that of the English Prayer-Book, and, therefore, sanctioned both by Convocation and Parliament, it is, nevertheless, in conflict with the researches which modern writers (and among them many distinguished English clergymen) have made into early Christian history. The late Dean of Westminster, after stating that during the first century and a half of the Christian era the words 'bishop' and 'presbyter' were used as convertible terms, remarks upon the diminished significance now attaching to the fierce controversy once waged between 'Episcopacy' and 'Presbyterianism.' 'It is as sure that nothing like modern episcopacy existed before the close of the first century, as it is that nothing like modern Presbyterianism existed after the beginning of the second. That which was once the Gordian knot of theologians has, at least in this instance, been untied, not by the sword of persecution, but by the patient unravelment of scholarship. No existing Church can find any pattern or platform of its government in those early days.'

The Divine right of episcopacy, as it has been called, *i.e.*, the theory that no priestly or ministerial authority can be bestowed except by means of the imposition of

---

[1] See Preface to the Ordination Service.

hands by a bishop or archbishop, was probably unheard of in the Reformed Church of England till the end of Elizabeth's reign. A few years before, Presbyterian ministers had lawfully held English benefices; but Divine right in ecclesiastical as well as in civil affairs was loudly asserted in the days of the Stuarts, and ultimately triumphed, when, upon the restoration of Charles II., the Act of Uniformity expressly stipulated that no one, unless *episcopally* ordained, should hold any ecclesiastical place, benefice, or promotion in the English Church.

No one can exercise any of the functions of any order of the ministry unless he has been ordained according to the form contained in the English Prayer-Book, or unless he has received episcopal ordination elsewhere. The orders bestowed by a bishop of the Episcopalian Churches of Scotland, Ireland, the British Colonies, or of the United States of America, are recognised as sufficient, and a clergyman belonging to any of those bodies would be permitted to officiate in this country, and to hold ecclesiastical preferment, upon taking and subscribing the oaths and declarations imposed upon the English clergy, and upon being duly licensed by a bishop of the Church of England. The orders, again, bestowed in the Roman Catholic Church are also so far recognised, that one of their clergy upon recanting his errors and joining the Established Church would be enabled to exercise the ecclesiastical functions without being re-ordained. The validity of the orders conferred by the Greek Church would probably be also recognised.

The admission into the ranks of the clergy, though regulated by law, is entirely in the hands of the bishops, and the lay power at no time asserted any claim to give ecclesiastical authority to those who have not first been received into one of the three orders of the Church. The ability to convey the spiritual authority to a minister is an incident of the episcopal character. Yet the making of a bishop is virtually the function not of any ecclesiastical authority, but of the Crown (as will be afterwards explained), acting upon the advice of a responsible Minister.

The regulations as to the admission into the different orders of the clergy have for their object to secure proper fitness in those who are to exercise the clerical functions; and we accordingly find strict rules laid down as to the age, character, orthodoxy, and learning of candidates for holy orders, and even further precautions taken intended to secure obedience of the clergy towards the bishop of their diocese and the law of their country. A deacon, in the absence of a faculty from the Archbishop of Canterbury, is required to be of at least twenty-three years of age; a priest must be twenty-four, and a bishop thirty; whilst as regards deacons and priests, only those are allowed to be ordained who can bring satisfactory evidence to the bishop of their moral character, of their education, and of their orthodoxy; and it is further provided that no candidate is to be admitted to holy orders unless he has provided himself with a sphere of duty in which to exercise his office, such for instance as that he has been nominated to some curacy, or unless he is a fellow of a college at Cambridge or Oxford, or is a Master of Arts of a certain standing resident at either University. Before ordination, moreover, every candidate is required to declare that he assents to the doctrine of the Church of England as set forth in the Book of Common Prayer and the Thirty-nine Articles of Religion; that he will use in the service of the Church the form of the Prayer-Book and none other, except in so far as it shall be ordered by lawful authority. He has to take the ordinary oath of allegiance to the Queen, and to swear 'that he will pay true and canonical obedience to his bishop and his successors in all legal and honest commands.' A deacon, when duly ordained, is qualified to act as an assistant to the priest, but is not endowed with an independent authority to perform the higher offices of the ministry, such as the pronouncing the absolution or the consecration of the Sacrament. To the office of deacon it appertains to assist the priest in Divine service and in the administration of the Holy Communion, to read the Scriptures in church, to preach if licensed by the bishop so to do, to baptize infants in the absence of the priest, and generally to assist the latter in the benevolent and charitable work of the parish; but on the other hand he is strictly forbidden by the statute law to hold any benefice, or to 'consecrate and administer the Holy Sacrament of the Lord's Supper,' under a penalty of 100*l*.

By the reception of priest's orders the deacon ultimately acquires from the bishop the full spiritual capacity to exercise the duties and functions of a Christian pastor; and, again, before receiving this second ordination, the candidate is required by the law to satisfy the same test of fitness, orthodoxy, loyalty, and willingness to obey his bishop, which we have seen were prescribed for the candidate for deacon's orders. The order of priests, thus constituted, forms the great body of the clergy, and with it specially rests the parochial and ordinary work of the Church. So irrevocably set apart from the rest of the community used the law to regard the clergy, that till the year 1870 it gave full effect even in temporal matters to the theory of the indelibility of orders,—'Once a priest always a priest,'—following the 76th Canon of 1603, which, upon pain of excommunication, forbids the minister to put off his spiritual character, 'or afterwards to use himself as a layman.' In former times the clergy constituted a separate order of the State, which was regularly convoked like the other orders of the State to aid the King with grants of supplies, being itself exempt from the taxation of Parliament. We have seen how in pre-Reformation days the clergy were exempt, to a great extent, from the jurisdiction of the ordinary tribunals of the country, the ecclesiastical courts having successfully endeavoured to widen their authority at the expense of the King's courts. The privileges of the clergy, however, are now-a-days not great, nor are their civil disabilities many; thus a clergyman is not liable to serve on a jury, neither can he be elected as alderman, town councillor, or member of Parliament; he cannot, while holding any religious office, enter into trade, nor without the written consent of his bishop may he farm more than eighty acres of land, under penalty of being deprived; neither probably would the general sentiment of other professions approve his admission among them as a member, while he still retained the position of a clergyman. Lately, however, his position has been improved, since by the Clerical Disabilities Act of 1870 any clergyman having first resigned any benefice, preferment, or dignity he may hold, may, by deed enrolled in Chancery, entirely divest himself of all the disabilities and privileges with which, as a clergyman, he had been clothed, and may free himself from the control of his bishop and from the jurisdiction of the ecclesiastical courts, and, in short, may for all purposes re-assume the legal status of a layman.

In the English system there are many gradations of rank from the Archbishop of Canterbury, Metropolitan and Primate of all England, down to the stipendiary curate. At the head of each of the two provinces of Canterbury and York, into which England and Wales is divided, is an archbishop, who is bishop of his own diocese as well as archbishop of his own province. The province of Canterbury has always been by far the more important of the two, though the growth of population in recent years in the North of England is being met to some extent by a strengthening of the northern episcopate, and hence the creation within the present reign of the three new Sees of Manchester, Ripon, and Liverpool, within the bounds of the province of York. And as the archbishop is the head of all the clergy within his province, so in each diocese is the bishop the head of all his clergy within it, with authority to *visit* every part of it in order 'to inspect the manners of the people and clergy,'[1] with power to ordain priests and deacons, to consecrate churches, and to confirm children. To the judicial authority of the archbishops and the bishops over the clergy it will

---

[1] Blackstone.

be necessary to refer when we deal with the ecclesiastical courts.

The two archbishops, and the Bishops of London, Durham, and Winchester, sit in the House of Lords. Of the remaining bishops only the twenty-one senior bishops are Lords of Parliament. The lords spiritual, thus consisting of twenty-six bishops, constitute one of the 'three estates of the realm,' whose assent is in theory required to give validity to an Act of Parliament. In practice the lords spiritual and temporal are merged, forming together the House of Lords, and the assent of each estate is not required. The bishops, though thus Lords of Parliament, are not in all respects upon the same footing as other members of the peerage. Their blood is not 'ennobled.' Therefore a bishop's wife is not a peeress, and a bishop, should he be charged with felony, is not to be tried by the House of Lords or by a jury of peers, but by an ordinary jury. The Bishop of Sodor and Man is not a spiritual peer.[1]

Subordinate to the bishop is the dean and chapter, constituting a corporation, the individuals composing the chapter, *i.e.* the canons,[2] being clergymen reserved for

[1] By virtue of a statute of Henry VIII. it is lawful to consecrate 'suffragan bishops' for certain towns named in the Act, and accordingly Bishops of Dover, of Nottingham, of Bedford, and of Guildford have been so consecrated. These 'suffragans' are appointed for the purpose of assisting the bishop of the diocese in the episcopal duties of his office. They are not spiritual peers of the realm, nor are they entitled to sit in the Upper House of Convocation.

[2] Each member of a chapter in a cathedral is now known by the title of 'canon. Such canons as have assigned to them for their support a fixed proportion of the cathedral revenue are called 'prebendaries.'—3 & 4 Vict. cap. 113, § 1.

the service of the bishop's cathedral from the general settlement made of the clergy through the different parishes of the diocese.[1] In the case of some *collegiate* churches, however, such as Westminster Abbey and the Free Chapel of St. George's, Windsor, the dean and chapter is found existing independently of cathedral or bishop.

Thus, at the cathedral or episcopal church of each diocese we find a complete establishment of cathedral clergy. Within the province of Canterbury are twenty-three dioceses—viz. Canterbury, London, Winchester, Oxford, Bangor, Bath and Wells, Ely, Exeter, Gloucester and Bristol, Hereford, Lichfield, Lincoln, Llandaff, Salisbury, Worcester, St. David's, St. Alban's, St. Asaph, Peterborough, Chichester, Norwich, Rochester, Truro.

And within the province of York are eight dioceses, —viz. York, Durham, Chester, Carlisle, Manchester, Ripon, Sodor and Man, Liverpool.

Another ecclesiastical dignitary (described in the old Canon Law as the Bishop's Eye), superior to the parochial clergy, is the *archdeacon*, an official appointed by the bishop, whose duty it is to *visit* the clergy within his archdeaconry originally as a kind of assistant of the bishop, but now as an officer of the Church invested with an independent authority of his own. Every diocese is divided into archdeaconries, and each archdeaconry into rural deaneries, but any judicial authority a rural

---

[1] The bishop is empowered to appoint 'honorary canons,' to come immediately after the actual canons in dignity, but who receive no pay and have no seat on the chapter.

Clergymen may be also appointed by the chapters (sometimes by the dean) to be 'minor canons.'

dean may have formerly possessed has now fallen into disuse.

Leaving now the dignitaries of the Church, we come to the rank and file of the clergy distributed throughout the whole country, upon whom mainly depends the active work of the Church, viz. the parish clergy, including rectors, vicars, perpetual curates, and assistant curates. To the rector, vicar, or perpetual curate belongs the 'cure of souls' of the parish. According to Blackstone, the rector is properly called 'a parson,' *persona ecclesiæ*, 'one that hath full possession of all the rights of a parochial church; and this appellation, however much it may be depreciated by familiar, clownish, and indiscriminate use, is the most legal, most beneficial, and most honourable title that a parish priest can enjoy.' The incumbent, whether rector, vicar, or perpetual curate, is generally bound by law to reside in his parish, unless his absence is permitted by the special licence of his bishop. To his duties, his position in the parish, and the provision made by law for his support, we shall have occasion hereafter to refer; at the present time it is sufficient to explain that the *vicar* came into existence in Roman Catholic days, in cases where the full rights of the rector to tithes and offerings had been *appropriated*, as it was called, by certain spiritual corporations, such as the monasteries. These bought up and acquired the advowsons, and obtained what were called appropriations of the benefices to themselves, and became thus in law themselves parsons of the parish; whilst in order to provide for the religious wants of the people they in some cases appointed a curate or deputy, who was called the vicar, at a stipend paid by the appropriators themselves, to perform Divine service and administer the sacraments. These vicars were gradually by statute law [1] given a more secure position, and vicarages received separate endowments, measures having been taken very early to prevent the parish from being starved of its ecclesiastical provisions by the greed of the religious houses. At the time of the Reformation it is said that one-third of the churches in England had been thus appropriated.

In some cases of appropriations not only the tithes and offerings of the rectory were appropriated, but in addition the appropriators acquired under the terms of the appropriation the cure of souls within the parish and performed the duties of the church by their own members. Where this was the case the above-mentioned statutes as to the endowment of vicars were considered not to apply, and no separate provision was ever made in favour of the officiating minister.

Upon the dissolution of monasteries and other religious houses under Henry VIII., the appropriations were by Parliament vested in the Crown; many of them were subsequently re-granted to subjects, and hence for the first time appear upon the scene 'lay impropriators,'

---

[1] Especially by statute 4 Henry IV. cap. 12, the object of which was to secure to the vicar permanency of position and sufficient endowment. The perpetual curate must be in priest's orders, as he has the 'cure of souls.' The assistant curate need only be a deacon.

It may be mentioned here that all incumbents of parishes where the churches have been built under Church Building Acts and who are not rectors, 'shall, for the purposes of style and designation only, be deemed to be vicars.'—31 & 32 Vict. cap. 117, § 2.

as they are called by the law, *i.e.* persons who own as their private property the tithes and endowments which once belonged to the religious houses.

Usually the lay impropriator acquired, in addition to the emoluments of the impropriate rectory, the right to present a clergyman to the vicarage on a vacancy occurring, and the presentee upon induction became entitled to the emoluments derived from the separate endowments of the vicarage. But where the religious house had itself possessed the cure of souls in the parish a *lay* impropriator was compelled to nominate some clergyman to take charge of the parish, and to pay him a stipend. Such clergymen and their successors are called perpetual curates. They must be licensed by the bishop, but they do not require institution or induction. Under a recent Act they have to make the same subscriptions and declarations as spiritual rectors and vicars.[1]

The rector, therefore, is the incumbent of a parish in full possession of all the parochial tithes and dues. *The vicar*, on the other hand, receives only a portion of the original emoluments of the parish, the rest having been appropriated. In modern times, owing to the growth of population, it has become customary in many parishes for the rector or vicar to obtain the assistance of one or more clergymen, who must be licensed for the work by the

---

[1] The 'perpetual curate' was not within the benefit of the Acts, but he is now no longer removable at the will of the impropriator, and practically his position as incumbent is similar to that of a vicar. It sometimes happens, however, that the patronage to a perpetual curacy is vested by ancient custom in the parishioners, who in that case elect their incumbent when a vacancy occurs.

bishop of the diocese. These are not entrusted with the cure of souls, nor have they any definite parochial position. Their duty is simply to assist the parish clergyman as *assistant-curates*.

We have now mentioned the various grades of the active clergy—the Church dignitaries, including archbishops, bishops, deans, archdeacons, canons, and the parochial clergy, whether rectors, vicars, perpetual or assistant curates; but there are many clergymen not on 'the active list,' so far as work of an ecclesiastical character is concerned, who must also be enumerated, such as fellows of colleges, schoolmasters, and teachers; while there are also many who are still in law clergymen, since they have been ordained, and have not divested themselves of their spiritual character, but who to most intents and purposes, so far as their occupations and habits of life are concerned, may be regarded as laymen.

The whole muster of the clergy for the year 1875 has been given in a tabular form as follows : [1]—

Church dignitaries	172
Incumbents holding benefices	13,300
Curates	5,765
Clergy in churches, &c.. . .	19,237
Schoolmasters and teachers	709
Chaplains, inspectors, &c.	465
Fellows of universities, missionaries, &c. . .	434
Unattached clergy	3,893
Other clergy	5,501
Total clergy	24,738

[1] Taken from the evidence of the Rev. Canon Ashwell, given before a Select Committee of the House of Commons on the 'Public Worship Facilities Bill, 1875.'

The clergy have in each province the right of meeting by their representatives in Convocation, an assembly which we have seen can be summoned, prorogued, and dissolved only by the sovereign, as supreme head of the Church. In the province of Canterbury Convocation comprehends two houses—the upper, composed of the archbishop and the bishops of dioceses within the province; and the lower, containing all the deans and archdeacons of the province, one proctor or representative sent up by each chapter, and two proctors elected by the parochial clergy of each diocese. In the province of York, however, both houses of Convocation sit together, and the two proctors representing the parochial clergy are elected by the clergy of each archdeaconry, instead of by the clergy of each diocese.

The object of the summoning of Convocation originally being the taxation of the clergy as an order, its constitution is unlike that of those Church councils, which in other countries have legislated for the Christian community. This assembly of the clergy differs essentially from those councils or synods composed wholly of *bishops* which, in accordance with the true Episcopalian theory, have met in other countries to declare the doctrines or the discipline of the Church. The laity, again, have no place in Convocation either directly or through representatives, as is the case in the governing councils of the Church of Scotland, where, in accordance with the Presbyterian theory of Church government, the clergy and laity meet and deliberate together. In the present day the authority of Convocation is extremely limited, its enactments being binding on the clergy only, and then only on condition of their having obtained the royal approval, and of being in conformity with the law of the land, which, incorporating, as it does, the whole of the Prayer-Book, leaves to Convocation little scope for indulging in ecclesiastical legislation.

From the year 1717[1] down to the present reign the practice was followed of proroguing Convocation by Royal authority immediately after it assembled in each year. Hence its power of discussion was withdrawn, as well as its power of legislation, down to our own time. Under the present practice discussion is permitted, but, except on a few occasions, the Crown has not allowed to Convocation any legislative authority.

[1] It was in this year that violent discussion arose over the writings of Dr. Hoadly, Bishop of Bangor, and it was due to the warmth of the 'Bangorian controversy,' as it was called, that the practice mentioned in the text was pursued.

CHAPTER IV.

CHURCH LAW AND CHURCH COURTS.

HAVING in the last chapter dealt with the composition of the Church, including clergy and laity, let us now turn to the laws by which the Church is governed and to the courts administering them. Every member of the Church, whether lay or clerical, is, of course, in the present day subject to the ordinary law of the land as administered in the regular courts of justice. It has long ceased to be possible for anyone to claim exemption from this jurisdiction by reason of any ecclesiastical privilege. The ecclesiastical person, whether bishop, dean and chapter, or parson of the parish, has his civil or temporal rights, just as the layman, be he Churchman or Dissenter, has. He owns property, he makes contracts, his own rights may be infringed, or he may infringe the rights of others. He thus may claim the protection of the civil courts and against him such courts may give redress. But besides what are recognised as the civil rights of every subject of the Crown, there exist certain other rights and relationships which have, or are supposed to have, a specially ecclesiastical character, and are, therefore, the subject of the ecclesiastical law. It is not long since all causes of a matrimonial and testamentary character were exclusively dealt with by the ecclesiastical courts. Marriage having been in Roman Catholic times treated as a sacrament, and long after the Reformation having been still considered as in the main a religious matter, questions arising out of this relationship naturally came to be dealt with by the spiritual courts. Testaments also fell within their exclusive jurisdiction, and so remained long after all testamentary causes, even in some Roman Catholic countries, were decided by the civil judge.

By the legislation of 1857 and 1858, however, questions of marriage, of legitimacy, and of divorce were withdrawn from the old jurisdiction, and the trial of testamentary causes from the old prerogative court of the Archbishop of Canterbury, and a new statutory tribunal, the Court of Probate and Divorce, was created.

There were some rights which might be enforced by either temporal or spiritual court—as, for instance, that of the parson of a parish, whether spiritual rector or lay impropriator, to tithes. But the temporal courts jealously guarded their jurisdiction even in such cases where a right of property was in dispute, insisting that they, with the assistance of juries, could alone judge of these.

So, again, with regard to a Church-rate duly imposed, the ecclesiastical courts had power to enforce its payment. But now, with regard both to tithes and Church-rates, the authority of the spiritual courts is practically withdrawn; for, as will be seen hereafter, a rent-charge has taken the place of tithe, which in cases of non-payment may be distrained for; and Church-rates have ceased to be enforceable at all, and have become nothing but mere voluntary payments by those who like to contribute to the maintenance of the fabric of the Church.[1] There may be other rights enforceable by suit in either ecclesiastical or civil court—as, for instance, the right of an incoming incumbent to claim damages from his predecessor for non-repair or injury suffered or done to the parsonage house. But in the present day it may be said with tolerable accuracy that the functions of the ecclesiastical courts are almost solely limited to maintaining—

1. The orthodoxy and discipline of the clergy;
2. The regulation of matters affecting church seats, the fabrics of the churches, and the churchyards;

whilst their authority over the laity has practically ceased to exist.

But though the jurisdiction of the *spiritual courts* is now so small, it would be a mistake to suppose that *ecclesiastical law* is non-existent; on the contrary, the common law of England recognises the ecclesiastical law, and in many a case before the ordinary courts of justice the rights of parties will still turn upon it. Thus in 1844 the House of Lords had to decide whether a marriage by a Presbyterian minister was a valid marriage at common law, or whether it must necessarily have been performed by a clergyman of the Church of England. To assist them to a conclusion great researches were made into the constitutions and canons of foreign and English councils and convocations, with the result that three of the learned lords held that such a marriage

---

[1] Though this is so as to newly imposed Church-rates, the Act for the Abolition of Church-rates, 1868, contained provisions preserving the old system in certain specified instances, generally of only local application.

was good, while three others held that it was no marriage at all.

The law governing the Church of England in any of its relations must be *Statute law, Common law,* as interpreted by the judges of the land, or the Queen's Ecclesiastical law, a portion of which is derived from Canon law, accepted in this country from abroad as being binding here, or which, being of English origin, owes its validity to Parliamentary sanction or to its conformity to the common law. The canon law is, in the main, founded on the civil law, *i.e.* the law of the Roman empire. As to the civil and canon law, 'their force and efficacy do not depend on their own intrinsic authority. They bind not the subjects of England, because their materials were collected from Popes or Emperors, were digested by Justinian or declared to be authentic by Gregory. These considerations give them no authority here; for the legislature of England doth not, nor ever did, recognise any foreign power as superior or equal to it in their kingdom, or having the right to give law to any the meanest of its subjects; but all the strength that either the Papal or Imperial laws have obtained in this realm is only *because they have been admitted and received* by immemorial usage and custom in some particular cases and some particular courts, or else because in some other cases they are introduced by consent of Parliament, and then they owe their validity to the statute law.'[1]

A certain distinction must be noticed between the older and more modern canons, for by the Act of Sub-

---

[1] Blackstone, *Commentaries.*

mission (25 Henry VIII.), revived in the first year of Elizabeth, it was enacted that 'such canons, constitutions, ordinances, and synodals provincial, *being already made*, which be not contrarient or repugnant to the laws, statutes, and customs of this realm, nor to the damage or hurt of the King's prerogative royal, shall now still be used and executed as they were afore the making of this Act, *till such time* as they be viewed, searched, or otherwise ordered and determined' by a commission of thirty-two persons to be appointed or provided by the Act. No authorised revision was ever made under these Acts, and hence the whole of the then existing Canon law, as limited by the clause above quoted, has statutory validity given to it. Canon law, however, of a later date stands in a different position. The question has arisen in connection with later ecclesiastical law how far the important canons of the year 1603, approved by the Crown, are of binding effect. Lord Hardwicke answers this on the general principles of the Constitution, viz. that they do not bind the laity. 'No new laws can be made to bind the whole people of this land, but by the King with the advice and consent of both Houses of Parliament, and by their united authority; neither the King alone, nor the King with the consent of any particular number or order of men, have this high power. To cite authorities for this would be to prove that it is now day. The binding force of these Acts of Parliament arises from that prerogative which is in the King as our sovereign liege lord, from that personal right which is inherent in the Peers and Lords of Parliament to bind themselves and their heirs and successors in their honours and dignities, and from the delegated power vested in the Commons as the representatives of the people; and therefore, Lord Coke says, they represent the whole Commons of the realm and are trusted for them. By reason of this representation every man is said to be a party to, and the consent of every subject is included in, an Act of Parliament; but in canons made in Convocation and confirmed by the Crown only, all these are wanting except the royal assent; here is no intervention of the Peers of the realm nor any representatives of the Commons.' Modern canons, however, as has been already explained in the last chapter, have a certain limited operation over the clergy. Practically, Parliament is the only ✓ authority which can legislate for the Church of England.

It is essential to the character of every Church that it should have a fixed creed. The limits of belief may be more or less wide, but limits there must be which divide it from other Churches and sects, and from unbelievers. Again, in each Church more or less uniformity in public worship is always required. It is a necessary condition of an *Established* or *State* Church that this creed and this form of worship and ritual should have the approval not only of its own actual members, but of the State itself.

When in 1772 an attempt was made by some of the clergy to be relieved from the necessity of subscribing the Thirty-nine Articles, Burke declared in the House of Commons: 'Nothing can be clearer to me than that forms of subscription are necessary for the sake of order, decorum, and public peace. By a form of subscription I mean a general standard, which obtains throughout the whole community, and not the partial creed of this or that bishop by whom a priest happens to be ordained. . . .' 'These gentlemen complain of hardships . . . let us examine a little what that hardship is. They want to be preferred clergymen in the Church of England as by law established, but their conscience will not suffer them to conform to the doctrines and practices of that Church; that is, they want to be teachers in a Church to which they do not belong, and it is an odd sort of hardship. They want to receive the emoluments appropriated for teaching one set of doctrines, while they are teaching another. A Church in any legal sense is only a certain system of religious doctrines and practices, fixed and ascertained by some law, by the difference of which laws different Churches (as different commonwealths) are made in various parts of the world; and the Establishment is a tax laid by the same sovereign authority for the payment of those who so teach and so practise. For no legislature was ever so absurd as to tax its people to support men for teaching and acting as they please, but by some prescribed rule. The hardship amounts to this, that the people of England are not taxed two shillings in the pound to pay them for teaching as Divine truths their own particular fancies.'[1]

---

[1] Nearly forty years later Lord Stowell used similar language in giving judgment against a clergyman proceeded against under the statute 13 Elizabeth, cap. 12, which enables the bishop to deprive any ecclesiastical person for advisedly maintaining any doctrine contrary to any of the Articles. To maintain that this was an obsolete Act was 'the idlest of conceits, for it was as much in force as any in the whole statute-book. . . . It was

Most people hold in the present day that it is for the good both of clergy and laity that the limits of orthodoxy should not be very rigidly drawn, and that a certain latitude of opinion should be allowed within the Church; but Burke's words remain, nevertheless, true in forcibly representing that what is taught by a State Church must be decided by the State, not by the clergy, nor even by the Church in the widest meaning of the word.

The procedure when charges are made against clergymen in the ecclesiastical courts for offences against the laws ecclesiastical is now regulated entirely by two Acts

essential to the nature of every Establishment, and necessary for the preservation of the interests of the laity as well as of the clergy, that the preaching diversities of opinion should not be fed out of the appointments of the Established Church; since the Church itself would otherwise be overwhelmed with the variety of opinion which must in each case arise out of the infirmity of our common nature. . . . What would be the state and conduct of public worship if every man was at liberty to preach from the pulpit of the Church whatever doctrines he may think proper to hold? Miserable would be the condition of the laity if any such pretension could be maintained by the clergy. As the law now is, everyone goes to his parochial church with a certainty of not feeling any of his solemn opinions offended. If any person dissents, a remedy is provided by the mild and wise spirit of toleration which has prevailed in modern times, and which allows that he should join himself to persons of persuasions similar to his own. But that any clergyman should assume the liberty of inculcating his own private opinions in direct opposition to the doctrines of the Established Church, in a place set apart for its own public worship, is not more contrary to the nature of an established church than to all honest and rational conduct. . . . It cannot, therefore, be maintained that the Church is liable to the reproach of persecution if it does not pay its ministers for maintaining doctrines contrary to its own.'

of Parliament passed in the present reign, viz. the Church Discipline Act of 1840 and the Public Worship Regulation Act of 1874. Therefore where proceedings are taken against clergymen for the promulgation of erroneous doctrine, disobedience to the rubrics and regulations of the Prayer-Book, immorality and drunkenness, brawling in church, unduly refusing to administer the Sacrament, &c. &c., these Acts must be strictly followed, and it in no respect ousts the jurisdiction of the ecclesiastical courts that the offence committed may be or has been the subject of an indictment at common law. Thus, where a clerk in holy orders had been tried and convicted of forgery, he was subsequently proceeded against in the ecclesiastical courts, which passed a sentence of deprivation. By the Act of 1840 the institution of proceedings depends upon the discretion of the bishop, who may, where a clergyman is charged with an offence, or who is the subject of public scandal, appoint five commissioners to inquire whether a *primâ facie* case appears to exist for taking further proceedings. Upon their report to the bishop, he may, if both parties to the suit consent, at once pass such sentence as the law authorises. If, however, a *primâ facie* case having been established, the bishop or the person complaining wishes to proceed further, articles of charge, specifying the offences alleged, must be drawn up and served upon the defendant, and his trial will then take place in the court of the bishop. The bishop, however, if he likes, may by letters of request send the case for trial at once to the court of the archbishop of the province. The dissatisfied party has the right of appeal from the court of the bishop to that of the archbishop, and from that of the archbishop to the Queen in Council.

This Act extends to *all* ecclesiastical offences committed by clergymen. The Act of 1874 is much less wide in its scope, as it only has reference to a limited class of offences, viz. the introducing unlawful ornaments or making unlawful alterations in the church, the using by the clergyman of unlawful vestments, or the neglecting to use those that are prescribed by law, and the non-observance of the directions of the Prayer-Book as to the ordinances, rites, and ceremonies therein ordered. The later Act in no respect alters the law, except as to procedure, its object being merely to simplify and shorten the procedure of the ecclesiastical courts when dealing with these specified offences. Proceedings under it, moreover, can only be taken by persons who have a special interest in the due observance of the law, namely, by the archdeacon, by one of the churchwardens, or by three parishioners of the parish. By consent of both parties the bishop, unless he is of opinion that further proceedings should not be taken, may, after considering all the circumstances of the case, give final judgment; but in case of a failure of consent, the bishop is to send the matter for trial at once to the archbishop of the province, who will transmit it to the judge of the provincial courts for his decision. The Act also empowers the parties to the suit to obtain the opinion of the judge upon legal questions arising in the course of the proceedings, and the judgment given by the bishop is to be in conformity with his opinion. It is left optional to parties complaining to proceed under either statute. As before, appeal lies to the Queen in Council.

But it is time now to explain what is the constitution of the three ecclesiastical courts we have mentioned, viz. the bishop's court, the archbishop's court, and the Privy Council, which have cognizance of ecclesiastical offences. The court of the bishop of the diocese, called also the diocesan court, or the consistory court, or court Christian, was the original court of first instance in the diocese, of which the bishop appoints the judge, the '*Judex ordinarius*,' by virtue of his office; whence he is called 'the Ordinary.' In this court the bishop himself does not preside in person, but by the judge so appointed by him, who is called his 'official principal,' or 'the chancellor of the diocese.' [1]

The archbishop's court, or the provincial court, is in the province of Canterbury known as the Court of Arches, so called because it was anciently held in the church of St. Mary *le Bow* (Sancta Maria de Arcubus), in the city of London, and in the province of York as the Chancery Court of York, and is presided over by the official principal of the archbishop. The Public Worship Act of 1874 makes a change in respect to the provincial courts, as it empowered the two archbishops, with the approval of the Crown, to appoint from time to time any person who has been a judge of the High Court of Justice, or a barrister of ten years' standing, being a member of the Church of England, to be judge

---

[1] By the Canons of 1603 a chancellor must be at least twenty-six years of age, and a Master of Arts or a Bachelor of Laws.

of the *two* provincial courts, and the judge so appointed was at once to succeed to the offices of official principal of the Arches Court and judge of the Chancery Court of York on vacancies occurring. Lord Penzance, who was appointed under the Act, has become under these provisions official principal of the Arches Court, and judge of the Chancery Court of York, and not merely 'the judge' under the Public Worship Act.

The ultimate court of appeal in all ecclesiastical cases is the Judicial Committee of the Privy Council, which since William IV.'s reign has taken the place of the Court of Delegates. The delegates were commissioners named by the King under the statute 25 Henry VIII. c. 19, which abolished appeals to Rome, but instead of these enabled 'the party, for lack of justice in the archbishop's court, to appeal to the King in Chancery;' and in all cases under the Church Discipline Act and Public Worship Act it is requisite to the constitution of the Judicial Committee that an archbishop or bishop be present at the hearing of the appeal.[1] The ecclesiastical courts have no authority to do more than *interpret* the law of the Church, such as they find it. They cannot declare what is true doctrine any more than

---

[1] Under the Appellate Jurisdiction Act of 1876 an Order in Council was issued in that year, providing that one of the archbishops or the Bishop of London, along with four other bishops to be appointed according to a certain rota, should attend as assessors at the hearing of ecclesiastical cases before the Judicial Committee of the Privy Council. When any ecclesiastical case is to be heard the five assessors for the time being are to receive a summons to attend, and *no such case is to be heard unless there be at least three of such assessors present at the hearing*. See Order in Council, November 28, 1876.

they can prescribe what are the rules of discipline or of ritual which the clergy must follow. These matters are determined by law, which it is their province to expound; and in cases of difficulty or doubt they show a wise tendency not to be over rigid in attaching a very definite construction to special or isolated expressions, drawn from the standards or regulations of the Church, without paying due regard to the general effect of these standards or regulations taken as a whole. We shall have occasion to notice later in this work that there is much in the nature of a compromise between conflicting views in the system of the English Church, and that Lord Chatham spoke with point when he referred to 'the Popish liturgy, the Calvinistic articles, and the Arminian clergy of the Church of England.'

The Privy Council has declared of itself that it is 'constituted for the purpose of advising Her Majesty in matters which come within its competency, but it has no jurisdiction or authority to settle matters of faith, or what *ought* in any particular to be the doctrine of the Church of England. Its duty extends only to the consideration of that which is by law established to be the doctrine of the Church of England, upon the true and legal construction of her acts and formularies, and it is not the duty of any court to be minute and rigid in cases of this kind.' If, therefore, a charge is brought against a clergyman of publishing false doctrine, the court must be clearly satisfied that the doctrine complained of, into the full meaning of which the court will inquire, is contrary to an *expressly declared* doctrine of the Church. Many points are left open to the private judgment of every

Churchman, and the Articles are not to be taken to contain the whole of Christian doctrine. Hence, upon a matter where the Articles are silent, or are ambiguous, each Churchman may hold his own opinion, unless the point is clearly decided by the rubric or formularies. It has upon such principles of interpretation been declared that it is not penal for an English clergyman to express a hope of the ultimate pardon of the wicked nor to teach that it is not the doctrine of the Church that every part of the Scriptures upon any subject whatever, however unconnected with religion or morality, was written under the direct inspiration of the Holy Spirit.

Interpretation, therefore, is the function of the Privy Council and of the other ecclesiastical courts. They do not presume to lay down doctrine on such questions as 'verbal inspiration,' or 'everlasting damnation,' but they do examine as to what are the doctrines *expressed* by the Church, and they interpret these upon the same rules of construction as are applied to the construction of statutes or written documents. The action of the courts is similar in many cases that have arisen in recent years on the much less important, though not less vexed, questions connected with ritual. Whether prostration by the clergyman before the elements is lawful, whether lighted candles should be allowed upon the Communion table, what dress should be worn, and on what occasions, by the officiating clergy, at what point of the compass from the table the clergyman should take up his position, what sort of bread should be used for the Communion, if, and how high, it should be elevated, what sort of tablecloth should be used to cover the Communion table, are all questions which have exercised the greatest legal intellects of the present reign. But no judge of the Privy Council has considered himself empowered with reference to these matters, to declare what in itself ought to be done. The inquiry has always been strictly limited to what has been prescribed by the Book of Common Prayer, or otherwise authorised as the law of the Church.

When it has been proved that a clergyman has committed the offence charged, the court proceeds to pronounce a sentence of greater or less severity according to circumstances. Generally speaking, where there has been misconduct the court may *admonish* the offender to abstain for the future from the conduct complained of; or it may *suspend* him from performing his clerical functions, and from receiving the emoluments of his benefice, and this suspension may be for a longer or shorter period; or it may *deprive* him of both office and benefice. Disobedience to an admonition renders the offender guilty of 'contumacy' or contempt of court, which is punishable with imprisonment until he has been absolved by the court. Under the Public Worship Regulation Act, disobedience to the monition of the court is followed by an order inhibiting the incumbent from officiating within the diocese for three months and until he undertakes to obey it in the future. If, however, the inhibition continues in force for three years, the benefice becomes void, and another incumbent must be appointed.

In case of non-residence, and in one or two other specified cases, the clergy are made liable by statute to special penalties, and to have a portion of their emoluments *sequestrated*, as it is called.

CHAPTER V.

PAROCHIAL SYSTEM.

We have seen in an earlier chapter how the whole country became divided into dioceses. These again became subdivided into parishes, each under the care of a resident clergyman. It is by the due working of the parochial system, by the energy and character of the parochial clergy, that the Church makes the importance of its work felt, and spreads its beneficial influence through the nation. For ecclesiastical purposes, a parish is that local area which is committed to the charge of one parson, or vicar, or other minister having care of souls therein. Though in its origin the parish was probably framed upon the old township, it soon became a purely ecclesiastical division, and the parochial officers were ecclesiastical also. The churchwardens with the parishioners in vestry assembled, presided over by the clergyman, managed the affairs of the parish and administered the parochial funds. Gradually the tendency increased to treat the parish, for purposes of local administration, as a civil as well as an ecclesiastical division; and it in particular acquired statutory authority to impose rates to provide for its poor and to elect officers to collect and administer the funds belonging to it; whilst on the parish from the earliest times the old common law had always imposed the duty of maintaining and repairing the public roads.

Thus the parish was of later origin than the diocese. Gradually the Church spread itself out from the cathedral cities, each of which constituted a nucleus from which fresh efforts were made ecclesiastically to conquer the country adjoining. As churches were built in one locality after another, the district adjacent to each became in time the parish. After the Norman Conquest no doubt many of the churches were built by the lords of manors; and it is still frequently the case that where there is a manor, the parish bounds and the bounds of the manor coincide, or that several manors are exactly included in one parish. It never happens that a manor contains more than one parish. Hence it has been thought that in such cases the lord of the manor must have made his tenants provide for the due service of worship in his church by making them specially appropriate their tithes in its favour, instead of paying them into a common fund to be distributed by the bishop of the diocese. In some of the larger parishes it happened also in early times that an additional church was founded for the accommodation of parishioners, known as a 'chapel of ease,' or chapel 'belonging to the mother church,' which chapel was sometimes used merely for Divine service; but in other places it was found invested with nearly all the privileges of a parish church. In either case the officiating minister of such a chapel is at common law the nominee of the incumbent of the parish, unless where the duties of the chapel are performed by the incumbent himself or the assistant curate.

The origin of these ecclesiastical divisions being of such ancient date, their boundaries could (until recently) only be determined by evidence of immemorial usage; and to perpetuate a due recollection of the parish limits there yearly took place the well-known 'perambulation of the bounds.' In the case of a disputed boundary at the present day, authority has been given by statute to the Inclosure Commissioners to inquire into the matter, and to set out and define the proper bounds of parishes, when they are engaged in enclosing common land. When first these ecclesiastical districts grew up round the newly founded churches, it is probable that the size of each depended to some extent upon the power of the minister and his church to provide for the religious requirements of the district. But where in many parishes population enormously increased, yet the religious establishment of the parish remained the same, it was found absolutely necessary to make further legislative provision to meet an inadequacy with which the occasional building of chapels-of-ease had proved itself quite unable to cope. Hence, at the beginning of the present century, it became the practice to pass Church-building Acts, by which in populous districts churches were established, and under the authority of which church-building commissioners divided and set out new parishes for all ecclesiastical purposes. These powers, still further extended, are now vested in the Ecclesiastical Commissioners, a newly established but most important corporate body, whose organisation and duties it will be necessary at another place fully to explain.

It may be roughly stated that the number of churches and chapels of the Church of England amounted in the year 1801 to between 11,000 and 12,000, in the year 1851 to between 14,000 and 15,000, and amounts at the present time to about 16,000; while we find that the number of ecclesiastical districts created since 1857, under statutory authority, amounted in 1874 to nearly 1,300. The incumbent, to use the most general term, whether rector, vicar, or perpetual curate, is the ecclesiastical head of the parish. Associated with him are two 'churchwardens,' parochial authorities appointed for a year by the minister and parishioners (that is, ratepayers of the parish) jointly; or who, in case the minister and his parishioners disagree, are appointed one by the minister and the other by the parishioners.[1] Minister, churchwardens, and parishioners constitute for ecclesiastical purposes the legal conception of 'the parish.' In the minister is vested the freehold in church and churchyard and the ecclesiastical profits of the parish for his life, or until his tenure is forfeited by non-fulfilment of the conditions imposed by law. Churchwardens,[2] remarkable as being the only laymen who are permitted to take any direct part with the clergy in business of an ecclesiastical character, are described by Blackstone as 'the guardians or keepers of the church and representatives of the body of the parish.' They are trustees of the moveable goods of the church, and their functions are to see to their proper

---

[1] It seems that the ordinary has a right to reject a churchwarden if the parishioners elect an improper person.

[2] Churchwardens were made overseers of the poor by the 43 Eliz.

maintenance, to the proper repair of the fabric of the church itself, and to preserve order during Divine service.

The method of appointment above mentioned is laid down in the 89th Canon of 1603, and in the modern parishes established by Act of Parliament the sanction of the legislature is given to the canonical system. So far, however, as the canons enjoin the churchwardens to act as censors of the morals of parishioners by reporting offences to the bishop they may be treated as having become obsolete. In order that the churchwardens might perform their legal duty of maintaining the fabric of church and churchyard, the parishioners in vestry assembled were entitled to impose a rate; and this was, in fact, the great function of the vestry considered in its ecclesiastical character. Church rates may still be imposed as before, but *the payment* of the rate has been made voluntary by the Church Rates Abolition Act of 1868, so that the parish vestry is now in ecclesiastical affairs an assembly enjoying an extremely limited authority.

Before anyone can fill the important place of parish clergyman, priest's orders must of course have been obtained, as without these no clergyman can be entrusted with the cure of souls. We have already shortly noticed the conditions and qualifications imposed by law on those seeking ordination. The priest thus duly ordained must in ordinary cases be *presented* by the patron of the living to the bishop of the diocese for his approval. The bishop, after examining the qualifications of the presentee, which is usually done by the bishop's chaplain, *admits* him if these are found sufficient, and then by *institution* commits to him the cure of souls within the parish. Subsequently, by *induction*, the presentee is actually put into legal possession of the temporalities of the benefice, in the same way as a purchaser of a freehold obtained the fee by actual 'livery of seisin.' When the bishop himself presents, presentation and admission become merged in one act known as collation. In some cases presentation, admission, and induction are all dispensed with, the appointment of the incumbent being made by the patron by simple deed. Such benefices are called *donatives*, and exist in cases where the patron, having founded a church, has, with the royal licence, kept it all to himself, free from the visitation of the ordinary. Though the incumbent's position resulting from either of these methods of presentation is that of freeholder for life, in parish church and churchyard, yet it is very much in the character of a *trustee* for the parish, since the common law gives every parishioner the right of using the church for purposes of Divine worship and the churchyard as a place of burial. The rights of the minister on the one hand, and of the people on the other, are of course mutually restrictive. The minister, for instance, may pasture the churchyard, but subject always to the right of any parishioner to have the pasturage broken up for the purpose of burial. The incumbent may authorise or refuse the erection of a tombstone, though his discretion on such a matter is liable to be overruled by the ordinary.

Whilst the church and the churchyard are thus put by the law at the service of any parishioner who may wish to use them, so also are the offices of the incumbent himself. He is a *public officer*, and it his duty as well as his privilege to baptize, to marry, and to administer the Sacrament, and other rites of the Church, to all who are lawfully entitled to claim them. This has always been the case at common law, and a recent statute has still further enlarged the public rights in the national churchyards by enabling those who have the right of burial to substitute for the Church of England burial service formerly obligatory, if any service were used at all, 'such Christian and orderly religious service as to their friends should seem best.'

Every step in the process of assigning a clergyman to his special field of labour is defined and regulated by law. The right of the patron to present is considered a right of property, and hence comes within the jurisdiction of the temporal courts; the right of the bishop to admit or refuse the patron's presentee is not one of mere discretion, for the bishop must have such reasons for his refusal as the law will approve. Not long ago a presentee duly presented (who had been for some years a parish clergyman) was refused institution by the bishop on the ground that his chaplain upon examination had found him *non idoneus et minus sufficiens in literaturâ*. The official principal of the Arches Court (Lord Penzance) held that the bishop was bound to show *in what* the presentee fell short of the lawful standard, so that 'the court might consider and decide whether the standard of learning set up by the bishop was such a standard as was required by law as a condition precedent to the clerk's right to be instituted.'

In order to secure the public services of the incumbent

the law provides against his residence out of the parish, or his absenting himself from it without the licence of his bishop for more than three months in any one year, by forfeiting in such cases a proportion of his income, and by preventing him in general from holding more than one benefice at the same time. But however careful the law may be in these respects, it is impossible for mere law to compel performance by a parish clergyman of the very indefinite but most important duties which he owes to his parish. He who is really worthy of his place will not be satisfied with conforming to mere legal or episcopal requirements. He has to befriend the poor and the distressed, to visit the sick, to appease quarrels, to keep his richer neighbours informed of cases where their assistance may be given to those who are less fortunate, and to point out the way in which this assistance can best be given. To this high standard of efficiency his own conscience can alone compel him. In popular parishes it is now usual for the clergyman to obtain the assistance of one or more curates, licensed by the bishop, in priest's or in deacon's orders, to whom he gives such a stipend as may be agreed upon, or, in cases where, from infirmity or other lawful cause, the bishop has seen fit to allow the incumbent to remain absent from his parish, a stipend regulated by Act of Parliament with regard to the largeness of the population and the parochial endowments.

It is impossible to over-estimate the importance to the country of the efficiency of this parochial organisation. Whether in the crowded parishes of our large towns, or in the remote districts of a thinly populated county, the clergyman should be the most useful of residents. In many districts he is often the *only* resident of any social position that the parish has to boast of, and still more often the only one whose avocations bring him into frequent relations with the poor. Whatever changes may come about in the course of time in the relationship of Church and State, there is no reason to fear but that in its main lines, a system of parochial ministration, from whatever sources it may draw its support, will be maintained.

It is striking to find the various aspects in which this position of a parish clergyman is regarded by the law. The 'cure of souls' one would suppose was 'a trust' of the highest importance, and upon this principle the law endeavours to guard against a clergyman for corrupt and selfish ends possessing himself of any benefice. Before a bishop is allowed to institute any presentee to a cure of souls, he must require the presentee not merely to take the oaths of allegiance and canonical obedience, but also to make a declaration that he has not 'made any payment, contract, or promise of any kind whatsoever, which to the best of his belief is simoniacal, touching the obtaining of his preferment.' Yet patronage, that is the right of appointing to these positions of trust, is as we shall see hereafter, treated by the law as the private property of the patron, which he may sell or mortgage, as his desires or necessities tempt him. And the distinctions between a simoniacal and a lawful contract we shall see are somewhat finely drawn. The incumbent when fully vested with the cure of souls may not divest himself of it without the consent of his bishop, and contracts entered into beforehand by which he was to vacate the benefice at some particular time, or in favour of some particular individual, were once held to be simoniacal, and therefore void; but now, by the statute law, 'resignation bonds,' as they are called, are valid, if made with the patron before presentation, binding the incumbent to resign *in favour of one of certain near relations of the patron!*[1]

Provision has also lately been made for allowing an incumbent to resign with the bishop's consent, on account of ill-health, and on certain other specified grounds, after he has been at least seven years in the benefice, on a pension of one-third of its revenues.

The position in which the incumbent finds himself as to remuneration, and the way in which this remuneration is provided, will have to be explained hereafter. In the main the tendency, since the times immediately following the Reformation, has been to improve both socially and pecuniarily the position of the country clergyman. From various causes he is now better paid than formerly, not only positively but also relatively to the general growth of rural incomes. His social position in the days of Charles II. is familiar to all who have read the brilliant chapter of Lord Macaulay describing the England of the Restoration, when the country parsons were chiefly persons no wealthier, and hardly more refined, than small farmers or upper servants, who thought it a treat to be invited to dinner in the squire's servants' hall, and who probably aspired to the hand of the lady's maid.

---

[1] 9 George IV. 94.

Complaints are sometimes heard in the present day of a falling off in the status of the clergy, but these, it may be hoped, are made by those who are always observing a falling off in much besides the clerical status. On the other hand, an eminent living writer tells us, in language sufficiently favourable to our modern clergy, that 'in England the accomplishments of a scholar and the refinement of a gentleman, blending with the pure and noble qualities of a religious teacher, have produced a class type which is rarely sullied with fanaticism, and is probably, on the whole, the highest, as it is the most winning, that has ever been attained.'[1]

The manner in which the beneficed clergy are remunerated, and the system by which clergymen are appointed to their livings, will be referred to hereafter.

[1] W. E. H. Lecky, *Rise of Rationalism in Europe*.

CHAPTER VI.

THE PRAYER-BOOK AND THIRTY-NINE ARTICLES.

We know that before the Reformation various liturgies were used in the different dioceses of England, and the present Prayer-Book, set forth in 1662, represents the last attempt made by the legislature to establish throughout the country a uniform liturgy and ritual in sympathy with the prevailing feelings of the people. Edward VI. found on his accession that these liturgies were numerous and tending to increase, and it was his object by the Book of Common Prayer to substitute for these different 'uses,' as they were called, one form of liturgy which should alone be sanctioned by Parliament. To this end he appointed Cranmer, Archbishop of Canterbury, to deliberate upon the matter with 'certain of the most learned and discreet of the bishops and other learned men of the realm.' The different service books were collected, translations from the Latin were made, prayers and ritual which seemed superstitious were omitted, and changes introduced wherever an alteration, in the opinion of the Commissioners, would bring the liturgy more into conformity with pure religion and the primitive usages of the Christian Church. The whole was then reduced to a single volume, now known as Edward VI.'s First Prayer-Book, which forms the basis of the one now in use. Whether this book ever received the approval of Convocation is uncertain; but Parliament gave it in the year 1549 its full sanction, and caused it to supersede as the sole religious service-book of the country, the ' Uses of Sarum, of York, of Bangor, of Lincoln,' and all the other liturgies then known in England.[1] A year later a form of service for the consecration of bishops, priests, and deacons was added, also by authority of Parliament.[2] The Puritan portion of the community, however, almost immediately began to express great dissatisfaction with the retention in the authorised worship of much of the distinctively Roman service and ritual, which had been discarded by the Protestants of the Continent, and which was generally distasteful to the more ardent reformers. In particular the retention of the very vestments worn by Romish bishops and priests in the celebration of the Mass as the lawful officiating dress of a Protestant ministry in performing the service of the Holy Communion, irritated the susceptibilities of a mainly Protestant nation. A desire, in which the King and his council thoroughly sympathised, for a simpler and more Protestant ritual being thus generally felt, the Prayer-Book was referred for revisal to a second Commission, consisting to a great extent of the same members who constituted the previous one. In the year 1551 this Commission finished its labours; and a revised Book of Common Prayer, now known as Edward VI.'s Second Prayer-Book, was published, which, having obtained the approval of Parliament, was made by Statute 5 & 6 Edward VI. c. 1, the sole

[1] 2 & 3 Ed. VI. c. 1.   [2] 3 & 4 Ed. VI. c. 12.

liturgy that might lawfully be used. By this new book vestments were abolished, and the surplice made the proper officiating dress of the parish clergy. The sign of the cross was no longer to be made in the Communion service in the consecration of the elements, nor was it to be employed in the celebration of marriage, nor in the Confirmation service; while a service for the exorcism of evil spirits contained in the First Book was entirely omitted in the Second. Prayers for the dead were likewise omitted, as was the name of the Virgin from those prayers in which it appeared among the names of the saints.[1] These changes show clearly enough the religious tendencies of those who substituted the Second for the First Book of Common Prayer. On the accession of Elizabeth it became necessary, in the first place, to put an end to the retrograde legislation of the intervening reign of Queen Mary, whose object it had been to re-establish the Roman religion. Her statutes concerning religion were accordingly repealed *en bloc*, and Elizabeth endeavoured to return to the state of things existing at the end of Edward's reign, and once more to establish a Protestant uniformity. Accordingly, Elizabeth's Act of Uniformity [2] enjoined the use of Edward's Second Book, into which were introduced a few slight modifications, and forbade under severe penalties any nonconformity with its provisions. Elizabeth's private sentiments, as is well known, inclined her to a ritual more elaborate than that

[1] The Sentences, Exhortation, Confession, and Absolution with which the service now begins first appeared in the Second Book. In the First Book, the service began with the Lord's Prayer.

[2] 1 Eliz. c. 2, A.D. 1559.

in favour with the majority of her subjects; and it is probably due to her personal predilections that, as regards the much-vexed question of vestments, no permanent settlement was effected by her Statute of Uniformity. This statute, as we have said, revived the more Protestant Second Book of Edward, but it nevertheless contained a proviso that the ornaments of church and minister which were prescribed by the less Protestant First Book of Edward should be retained until fresh regulations were made on the subject in the manner specified in the Act. A few years later this was done upon the advice of the Archbishop of Canterbury and several of the bishops appointed Commissioners for Ecclesiastical Causes under the Great Seal, by the issue of regulations duly sanctioned by the Queen, called the 'Queen's Advertisements,' for the purpose of ensuring due order in the public administration of the common prayers, and 'partly for the apparel of all persons ecclesiastical.' These Advertisements, which rendered the use in parish churches of vestments other than the surplice illegal, were rigidly enforced; and having been issued in pursuance of an Act of Parliament, were thus made part of the law of the land, and, except so far as affected by later legislation, still remain law. It is worthy of notice that Elizabeth's Act of Uniformity, which passed after the most strenuous opposition in Parliament, was opposed by the whole bench of bishops, and that it expresses itself as having been enacted 'with the assent of the Lords and Commons in Parliament assembled,' instead of using the more common form of the 'Lords *spiritual* and temporal in Parliament assembled.'

In the reign of Elizabeth, while the liturgy was thus

assuming the shape it now bears, the Articles of Religion, which, to the number of forty-two, had been first published by Convocation in 1552, were also reduced to their present shape and number. In 1571 they were finally approved by the Queen and Convocation, and were so far sanctioned by Parliament that subscription to such of them as affected true Christian faith or the doctrine of the sacraments was made compulsory on all ministers of the Church.[1]

Upon the accession of James I. was published a very important code of regulations, which had been drawn up by Convocation, and was duly authorised by the King, viz., the Constitutions and Canons Ecclesiastical of 1603. These canons, having never been confirmed by Parliament, in accordance with principles which have been already referred to, are binding only on the clergy, and only so far as they are not repugnant to the general law of the land. For the most part they were framed upon pre-existing canons, and they give full recognition and acceptance to the Book of Common Prayer as then authorised by Parliament.

It is, however, the Act of Uniformity of Charles II. (13 & 14 Car. II. c. iv.) which in the main defines the present position of the Established Church. So far as that Act imposed disabilities and penalties for non-conformity, it has indeed undergone much change; but it still remains the governing statute which regulates the lawfulness of doctrine and worship in the National Church. Immediately after his restoration King Charles had appointed under the Great Seal a commission of bishops

---

[1] 13 Eliz. c. 12.

and other divines once more to review the Prayer-Book, and to make such alterations as they thought expedient. When this had been done the King further submitted the revised book to the Convocations of the two provinces for their approbation. Finally, in the year 1662, Parliament gave its approval, 'annexing and joining' the Book of Common Prayer to the Act of Uniformity. This original book was in manuscript, and in the year 1819 it is known to have been still among the Parliamentary records, but for many years afterwards it was entirely lost sight of, in spite of diligent search repeatedly made for it. It was recently discovered almost by accident, and is now in the keeping of the House of Lords. Under the Act the various cathedrals and collegiate churches in England and Wales were to be provided with true printed copies of this book, exemplified under the Great Seal of England; and copies similarly exemplified were also to be kept at the Tower of London, in the Court of Chancery, and at Westminster Hall in each of the Courts of Queen's Bench, Common Pleas, and Exchequer; and these 'sealed books,' as they are called, are made by the Act itself 'as good records' as the manuscript book actually annexed thereto. The Prayer-Book of 1662, with its rubrics, is therefore part of the statute law. It contains the whole of the Liturgy, Psalter, Creeds, the Services for Baptism, Marriage, Burial, Consecration and Ordination of Bishops, Priests, and Deacons, and for other occasions. The Thirty-nine Articles do not form part of the sealed books, but owe their position as a standard of the Church to other independent authority.'[1]

[1] They were recognised by Charles II.'s Act of Uniformity, as well as by 13 Eliz. c. 12.

Thus there have been three Books of Common Prayer recognised by Acts of Parliament, which, in accordance with the desire for uniformity of worship, the legislature has endeavoured exclusively to impose upon the nation—

1. The First Prayer-Book of Edward VI.

2. The Second Prayer-Book of Edward VI., differing considerably, and in the Puritanical direction, from the former one; and which itself received a slight modification in one or two passages by Elizabeth's Act of Uniformity.

3. The Prayer-Book of 1662; by conformity to which in the present day questions of orthodoxy, of doctrine, of worship, and of ritual are tried.

The spirit of compromise which has always been characteristic of the Church of England is very conspicuous in its Prayer-Book, whose framers must have sought to comprehend within the fold of the Church Protestants of various descriptions, whether leaning to Calvinistic doctrine on the one hand or to an almost Roman ritual on the other. And in the desire to effect a wide comprehension, the Prayer-Book and the formularies of the Church are still expounded by the Ecclesiastical Courts, carrying out, in short, the views expressed in the Preface first prefixed to Edward's Second Book, and still retained, viz., 'that it hath been the wisdom of the Church of England, ever since the first compiling of her public liturgy, to keep the mean between the two extremes, of too much stiffness in refusing, and of too much easiness in admitting, any variation from it;' for as, on the one hand, some changes have done more harm than the mischief they were meant to cure, 'so on the other side the particular form of Divine worship and the rites and ceremonies appointed to be used therein, being in their own nature indifferent, and **alterable and** so acknowledged, it is but reasonable' that such changes as may be deemed expedient should be made by the proper authority.

However, from that day to this, though nearly two centuries and a quarter have passed away, the Book of Common Prayer has remained almost entirely unchanged; the Book annexed to the Act of Uniformity and the sealed books are still the standard; and though there can be no doubt that orthodox members of the Church of England in 1882 differ in many respects from orthodox Churchmen of 1662, the letter of the law remains almost the same. The Prayer-Book and all its contents, and the Thirty-nine Articles, are alike beyond the reach either of the royal supremacy or the authority of ecclesiastical councils. The only loophole through which alteration might creep in would seem to be the proviso of section 25, which permits in all the prayers affecting the King, Queen, or Royal progeny, a change of name to be made by 'lawful authority' to suit the necessities of the time; this authority in the present day being a royal command under counter-signature of the Secretary of State. Nevertheless, in spite of the strictness of the statute, and in spite of the oath taken by every clergyman to use the form of the Prayer-Book 'and none other,' except so far as lawfully authorised, it has been usual to add by royal authority special prayers and special services on suitable occasions. In this way a day of solemn fast was ordered, and a service provided, during the national troubles caused by the Indian mutiny, and a day of thanksgiving for the peace at the end of the Russian war.

Even services intended to be permanently used have been added without dispute to the Prayer-Book, and for centuries have had the full sanction of the law. The Service of Thanksgiving for the Happy Deliverance of King James and the Three Estates of England from the bloody-intended massacre of the Gunpowder Treason; the Service of Prayer with Fasting on the day of King Charles the Martyr, and the Service of Thanksgiving for the Restoration, are none of them contained in the sealed books. The religious observance of those days was enjoined by Act of Parliament, but the services were framed in pursuance of the royal command, and added to the Prayer-Book.[1] The service for June 20, the accession of the Queen, was published by her command the very day after her accession, under the signature of Lord J. Russell, the Secretary of State. The usage, therefore, is thoroughly recognised of adding when required by royal command special services or prayers to the ordinary services of the Church; such services or prayers being in practice framed by the Archbishop of Canterbury. In 1859 both Houses of Parliament addressed the Queen against the further observance of January 30, May 29, and November 5, and in consequence a statute was passed repealing the Acts relating to these days, and subsequently by royal command the services for St. Charles the Martyr, the Restoration, and the Gunpowder Plot were ordered to be omitted. We may take it, therefore, that the Act of Uniformity and the oath required by the clerical Subscription Act should be understood in a somewhat

---

[1] This service was framed upon that published by Queen Anne.

limited sense, viz., that no prayers or services should be used in substitution of those prescribed by the Prayer-Book, leaving it in the power of the Sovereign to make in the proper manner such additions as from time to time might seem desirable.

In the present reign two statutes have been passed, namely in the years 1871 and 1872, which have made certain modifications in the Prayer-Book of 1662. The Prayer-Book (Tables of Lessons) Act and the Act of Uniformity Amendment Act have rearranged the Lessons, or portions of Scripture to be read at morning and evening service, and provided a shortened form of service instead of the full service formerly prescribed. The passing of the latter Act through Parliament, followed (as did the Act of 1662) the report of a Royal Commission appointed to consider the matter; and the consideration of the subject had also been referred by the sovereign to Convocation. The precedent of 1662 in the Act of Uniformity was thus closely followed in the Act of Uniformity Amendment Act, 1872. The stages were, first, reference of the matter to a Royal Commission for report; secondly, submission of this Report to Convocation; thirdly, legislative sanction. While the statute law has thus received some slight amendment, the canons of the Church of England have also in our own time undergone modification, though of no very great importance; for in the year 1865 the Convocations of the two provinces, under licence from the Crown, framed four new canons instead of the 36th, 37th, 38th, and 40th of those of 1603. The object sought was to bring the canons imposing oaths and declarations on those about to enter the ministry into conformity with the requirements of the Clerical Subscription Act of that year. These new canons were subsequently promulgated by the Crown.

We have seen in an earlier chapter [1] how the Church is governed by statute law, common law, and ecclesiastical law. The first, where it is found explicit, prevails over the other two. Several of the principal statutes affecting the position of the Church have already been referred to, including the Acts of Uniformity of Edward, Elizabeth, and Charles II. The common law is that which is expounded as law by the judges of the temporal courts, either as being the result of cases already decided, or as being deduced from accepted principles, or as being consistent with recognised usage.

The ecclesiastical law is that law which is administered in the ecclesiastical courts, and consists in part of such canons and constitutions ecclesiastical as have been allowed by general custom within the realm. As so laid down, it forms the 'Queen's Ecclesiastical Law.'

Among the sources from which the Queen's ecclesiastical law is derived may be mentioned the ecclesiastical constitutions enacted in the national synods presided over by Papal legates in the reign of Henry III., and the canons enacted from time to time by the Convocation of Canterbury, and accepted as a whole under Henry VI. by the province of York, and also such foreign canon law as was formerly accepted in this country. The great depository of such portions of the canon law as ever acquired any force in England is the collection of Lyndewode. The validity of so much of it is

[1] Ante, p. 40.

recognised by Statute 25 Henry VIII. as before mentioned.[1] Finally, there is the modern canon law, such as the Canons of 1603, as amended in 1865. Besides these sources of law notice must be taken of those regulations due to royal authority. Such are the injunctions of Edward VI., the injunctions of Elizabeth, and the advertisements of Elizabeth. The latter have been already mentioned, and appear to owe their authority in part to a provision of the Act of Uniformity, 1 Elizabeth, c. 2; while her injunctions and those of Edward, whether their issue was or was not originally within the authority of the Crown would probably be now taken as law where their prescriptions had been obeyed, and where they have not been repealed by subsequent Acts of Uniformity or other statutes.

Thus, to sum up the results of this chapter, we find the position and character of the National Church carefully defined, first of all by Acts of Parliament which authorise and incorporate the Prayer-Book and give a sanction to the Articles of religion. Next, we find in existence and of more or less authority, first, a body of church law; and, secondly, a collection of royal edicts issued by Edward, Elizabeth, and James I. Thirdly, we find added to the Prayer-Book by royal authority in accordance with recognised usage, such special prayers and services as from time to time the necessities of the country have seemed to require. And, last of all, we have common law, based in the main upon usage and interpreted by the judges of the civil or ecclesiastical courts.

[1] Ante, p. 44.

CHAPTER VII.

THE REVENUES OF THE CHURCH.

It is necessary to point out, before inquiring into the endowments of the Church and the provisions made for its support, that 'the Church' as a whole is, strictly speaking, not the owner of any property at all. It is not a corporate body capable of holding land or other property. As we have seen, the Church includes laity as well as clergy; but, in this wide yet true meaning of the word, it is without organisation, and its limits have never been legally determined. It is true that the clergy are, unlike the laity of the Church, a well-defined body of individuals; and though they once constituted an order of the State, with many more rights and privileges than they now possess, they do not, nor did they at any time, constitute a corporation in the eye of the law. The priesthood as a whole was always incapable of owning property, though the different persons of which that order was composed might own or acquire property, under the conditions prescribed by the law, which from time to time has undergone considerable changes with reference to this subject.

The Church *includes* a large number of corporations, without being a corporation itself. When people speak of the wealth or the estates or the revenues of 'the Church,' they mean the whole of the wealth, estates, or revenues belonging to the different ecclesiastical corporations included with it. Each bishop, dean, and chapter, or parson of the parish, is a distinct corporation, with extensive rights of property; but there is no body of persons known to the common law capable of owning property on behalf of the Church at large.[1] When, therefore, we speak of the property of 'the Church,' we mean the ecclesiastical wealth of the country shared among the different ecclesiastical persons whom we have already mentioned. The dean and chapter or the parson hold lands and tithes, just as any other corporation, aggregate or sole, may hold them; that is, they hold 'to them and their successors,' instead of 'to them and their heirs,' like the lay owner of an estate in fee simple. No outside authority, with the exception of Parliament, can affect these proprietary rights. The life estate of the incumbent in his glebe and tithes, is as entirely beyond the reach of any action of bishop or church-council, so long as he does not seek to alienate it, as is the squire's in his paternal acres; though, unfortunately, the general use of the expression 'Church property' has made common a belief that there is a sort of general ownership on the part of the Church, which, in fact, has no existence.

Having warned our readers against the danger of misapprehension of this convenient way of describing the ecclesiastical wealth of the country, we may point out that the revenues of the Church of England are derived from the rents of land, from fines on renewals of leases of Church

---

[1] See chap. viii.

estates, from glebe and augmentation lands, from tithes now converted into a rent-charge, from surplice fees, from pew rents, and from some other sources of inconsiderable emolument.[1] The income derived from pew rents is no part of the ancient ecclesiastical revenues, as in all old parishes every parishioner has a common law right to a sitting in the parish church without payment. As we shall see hereafter, pew rents are of modern origin, being part of the system introduced during the present century by the Church Building Acts. In the main, therefore, the wealth of the Church consists in the present day of lands and of the tithe rent-charge; and it is now time to explain the position of the Established Church in relation to these very valuable endowments. Both were acquired in very early times; but there is this very important distinction between them, namely, that the landed estates are due to Royal and private benefaction, for no general territorial endowment of the Church was ever made by law; while the tithes were a legal provision expressly made for the maintenance of the national religion.

The extensive estates that came into the possession of the Episcopate, and of the deans and chapters, prove the generosity and piety of the sovereigns of England and the more wealthy among their subjects. We have already seen how, at the time of the Reformation, one-fifth of England was in the hands of the religious houses; and long before that date the growing extent of Church lands had alarmed the King and Parliament. It was during the two centuries following the Norman Conquest that the largest alienations of lands to the ecclesiastics took place,

---

[1] See *Revenues of the Church of England*, by Rev. M. Cove.

these lands thereby becoming freed from feudal services, from contributing to the defence of the country, and from the liability to forfeiture and escheat; events which would again have brought them into the hands of the king or feudal lord. Alienations 'in mortmain,' therefore, being opposed to the interests of the King and nobility, were forbidden by Parliament, which enacted that grants of land to the religious houses, and afterwards to other religious corporations, such as the bishops, should be void, unless made with the royal license. In feudal times this ecclesiastical tenure of land was of two kinds, one known as frankalmoigne or free alms, the other as tenure by divine service. The tenure of frankalmoigne was the only tenure to which no fealty or services attached, whilst when lands were held by tenure by divine service the only duty the tenants had in general to perform was fealty and the saying of prayers for the souls of the donor and his heirs, which the law considered a higher service than that of any of the ordinary feudal tenures.[1] It was by one or the other of these tenures that the old monasteries and religious houses held their lands, and by tenure of frankalmoigne the parochial clergy hold their glebes at this day. Against the stringency of the Mortmain Acts the ecclesiastics struggled for a time with great ingenuity and with considerable success; but the general principle insisted upon by Parliament ultimately prevailed—that without a license from the Crown, lands could not be acquired by the Church. Other statutes have forbidden the alienation of land *by* the Church; but in modern times, for the sake of convenience, several exceptions

---

[1] Blackstone.

have been introduced to this general principle of the inalienability of land, whether by or to ecclesiastical 'persons.' Thus, much attention has recently been given to the important object of improving the position of the parish clergy. Hence a grant of land, to form an addition to the incumbent's glebe, may be made, though only to the extent of a very limited number of acres. And, in order to improve the residence houses of the clergy, the restriction on alienation is further relaxed; for the bishop or the incumbent has under certain circumstances authority to raise the requisite funds by burdening the benefice.

Two important corporations, to which reference will be made hereafter, viz. the governors of Queen Anne's Bounty and the Ecclesiastical Commissioners, now exist, through whose intervention lands may be granted for ecclesiastical purposes and in favour of a special benefice. Under the Church Building Acts, new ecclesiastical districts were allowed to be endowed with lands by benefactors to the value of 300*l.* a year. Provisions have also been made to facilitate exchanges of Church lands. All these statutory provisions, however, merely prove the generality of the rule to which they form exceptions. And the law still, subject to these exceptions, forbids the indiscriminate granting of lands without the license of the Crown, either in favour of any benefice or for the endowment of any ecclesiastical corporation.

Whilst the Church lands, or at least by far the greater portion of the landed estates, were owned by the dignitaries of the Establishment, viz. by the bishops and the deans and the chapters, the tithes and the glebes formed the great provision for the maintenance of the parochial clergy. As regards the management and distribution of the episcopal and the capitular estates, immense changes have taken place in the last half-century, as a consequence of the extended enquiries into the whole subject of Church revenues, which began in 1832. From this time dates a centralising tendency in the management of the affairs of the Church, which, however essential to its obtaining the full use of its resources, is entirely foreign to its original constitution and the fundamental principles of its government.

Tithes are defined as being 'the tenth part of the increase yearly arising and renewing from the profits of lands, the stock upon lands, and the personal industry of the inhabitants.' The first kind, such as those of crops and wood, were called prædial tithes; the second, as of wool, milk, pigs, &c., being partly the natural produce, and partly due to the keeping, industry, and diligence of the owner, were called mixed tithes; while the last kind was known as personal tithes, being the tenth part of the profits of certain trades and fisheries, and being exigible only by special custom where they were claimed, and not by the common law. Prædial and mixed tithes were the tenth part of the *gross* produce, while personal tithes, when claimable, were the tenth part of the *net* proceeds of the occupation. Tithes are generally classed under the division of great tithes and small tithes; the prædial tithe of hay, corn, and wood being included under the former, and personal tithes under the latter head. This classification is of importance; for where there are appropriations, *primâ facie*, the rector is held entitled to the great and the vicar to the small tithes.

Hence it often happens that very poor livings are found in combination with the finest and largest parish churches, which, in the days before the Reformation, had belonged to some wealthy abbey or priory. But now the scale of the endowment is no longer proportionate to the magnificence of the Church, the great tithes, on the suppression of the old religious houses, having been acquired, and being still enjoyed by some layman, who, so far as parochial endowments are concerned, is in law the rector of the parish.

Thus tithes were in the main a tenth of *the increase* from the land. However valuable the land might be, as, for instance, from its mineral wealth, if the value was not derived from *increase*, it was not titheable. In times when agriculture was much more exclusively the business of the nation than it has since become, the tithe represented a large proportion of the annually produced wealth of the whole country; while in the present day the rent charge, which represents tithe, falling almost entirely upon agricultural land, leaves uncharged the most valuable land in the kingdom, i.e. the town land and the mines. The owner of a thousand acres of land in the country finds it burdened with what is, compared with the rental of the land, a heavy charge to support the National Church; whilst the owner of an equal area in the colliery districts, though he may only contribute a sum in proportion to the yearly income he would have received if his property had been agricultural land, pockets a rent roll of perhaps many thousands a year. Up to 1836 tithe was payable in kind, or by special composition in lieu of it. It was the business of the farmer to set aside every tenth sheaf of corn for the tithe owner, so that a comparison might be made between that and the nine-tenths which were his own share. With regard to milk, it was settled that it should be tithed by the giving up of the whole milking of every tenth day; while the method of tithing wool, the young of cattle, sheep, &c., was also laid down. Some crops of modern introduction, such as flax and hemp, were, on the other hand, tithed under Act of Parliament at a fixed rate of so much per acre. But the characteristic of common law tithe was that it was the tenth of the increase, and was payable by the cultivator in kind; and so it generally remained till the Tithe Commutation Act of 1836.[1]

This magnificent provision by tithes for the support of religion was of no very early institution in Christian countries. It does not appear to have been known before the end of the fourth century; but its adoption throughout Christendom at length became general. In all countries ecclesiastics were enthusiastic in its support, and united in prescribing to their Christian flocks a strict obedience to the Divine command, contained in the Mosaic law, to the children of Israel. 'All the tithe of the land, whether of the seed of the land or of the fruit of the tree, is the Lord's;' and the same rule was applied

---

[1] In the City of London, and in some instances in other large towns, the tithes or annual amounts payable in lieu of tithes are regulated by the provisions of local Acts of Parliament. The payments in lieu of tithes in the City of London are, except in the cases of a few parishes, outside the provisions of The General Tithe Commutation Acts, and although now commuted in, it is believed, every instance for a fixed annual sum, were originally, except when a less rate was payable by custom, 2s. 9d. in the £ on the rental.

to the flocks and the herds by the same law.[1] An authority and antiquity such as this might seem sufficient; yet it did not satisfy the more ardent admirers of the institution. One of them, in a work full of information, to which reference will often be made hereafter, preferred to attribute it to a still earlier period in the world's history—in fact, to the earliest period of which the nature of the case will permit. Dr. Morgan Cove, Prebendary of Hereford, in his 'Essay on the Revenues of the Church of England,' writing in 1816, suggests that the institution of tithe must have been contained 'in some unrecorded revelation made to Adam, and by him and his descendants delivered down to posterity.' But, laying aside mere theory founded upon the keen appreciation of its intrinsic merits, the tithe system in England undoubtedly dates from the earliest times. The payment of tithe was ordered in this country by ecclesiastical councils at the end of the eighth century; and on the continent of Europe, at about the same time, was prescribed by an ordinance of Charlemagne, which appropriated it in four portions—to relieving the poor, maintaining the fabric of the church, supporting the bishop, and endowing the parochial clergy. In the middle of the ninth century a general council for the whole of England, lay and ecclesiastical, was held at Winchester, at which were present the various kings and magnates of the land; and by this assembly a general tithe was ordered to be levied in perpetuity for the maintenance of religion. Thus the claim of the Church to tithes is older than the monarchy. In England the tithes seem to have been

---

[1] Leviticus xxvii. 30-32.

originally paid to the bishop for distribution among the clergy of his diocese, though it was permitted to the tithe-payer to select the ecclesiastical recipient of his tithes. After the Conquest, the lords of manors in many cases secured the payment of tithes within the manor to the support of the nearest parish church, while in other cases they were paid to the religious houses, no doubt usually on condition of the latter performing masses for the souls of their benefactor and his heirs. This practice of the arbitrary consecration of tithes, as it was called, becoming very common, threatened to withdraw from the parochial clergy the provision intended for their support. It was, therefore, forbidden, with the authority of the Pope, in the time of King John; and now for many centuries the tithe has been regarded as being *primâ facie* the lawful provision made for the parson of the parish.

Thus from a very early period the land was burdened by the law with the charge of providing for the parochial clergy. Still some land was exempt; for that which produced no profit was not titheable by reason of its unproductiveness; while lands owned by the religious houses were also held free from the charge, a freedom which, when the impropriation to private purposes of the abbey lands took place at the Reformation, the King and the Parliament showed themselves anxious to preserve.[1] Hence it is still the case that lands which were once abbey lands are not liable to tithe.

[1] 31 Hen. VIII. c. 13 provided that persons coming into possession of abbey lands should hold them discharged from all tithes, as they had been when belonging to the suppressed religious houses.

It is evident that the general acceptance of the principle of tithe would enable the clergy to claim their proportion of produce, though arising from crops unknown to the country at the institution of the tithe system, as also from land which only the advance in the knowledge of agriculture had at length been able to render profitable. The cultivation of hemp and flax, turnips and potatoes, was not known in England till centuries after the tithe of corn and grass had been imposed. Nevertheless the Church was entitled to its tenth in kind, or to some fixed payment in lieu of it. How small an extent of England was under cultivation even three centuries ago writers have endeavoured roughly to estimate. A statute of Edward VI. impliedly provided that barren and waste ground, which had hitherto paid no tithes by reason of its barrenness, should, after conversion into arable or meadow, be still exempt from the burden of tithes of corn and hay till seven years had elapsed from the completion of the improvement. By the common law such land would have become titheable immediately; and no doubt the statute was passed to limit the discouraging effect which such a law must have produced on agricultural improvement. Thus it is that in consequence of the imposition of tithe upon new products, and its extension to new lands, the parochial endowments of the Church are at the present day in great measure drawn from sources which were not fully available to the clergy of earlier times. It has been calculated that no less than three-fourths of the cultivated land of England has been reclaimed since the above-mentioned statute of Edward VI.; and, though possibly this may be an over-estimate, there can be no doubt of the immense extension of agriculture that has taken place.[1]

The inconvenience of levying in kind from the cultivators of the soil a tenth of its produce at length induced Parliament to substitute a rent-charge for the tithes formerly payable. It was a further objection to the tithe that, being a fixed proportion of the *gross* produce, it took no account of the increased expenditure which could alone render a larger produce obtainable from the land. The whole *profit* due to the farmer's increased outlay might be swept away by the tithe-owner.

In modern times, even before the passing of the general Act, a money composition was, in practice, paid in most parishes instead of tithes in kind. This was under the authority of private Acts of Parliament, of which some two thousand are said to have been passed, or by virtue of agreements made between the tithe-owner and the tithe-payers. The former, however, if a spiritual rector or vicar, could not bind his successors by such an agreement; so that, on an incumbency being vacated, it often happened that uncertainty and dispute arose as to the amount claimable.

In the year 1836, therefore, the Tithe Commutation Act was passed, with the object of fixing once for all the burden to which lands were subjected, and of substituting a regular money payment for the inconvenient payment in kind. Commissioners were appointed to calculate the average value of tithes, or of the composition in lieu of them, in each parish of England during the preceding

[1] See *Title Deeds of the Church of England*, by the late Mr. Edward Miall, 5th edit.

seven years, and upon this basis to commute the tithes into an annual money payment, which, however, was to vary with the current price of corn. Payment was to be half-yearly, and each payment was to be the value at existing prices [1] of the amount of wheat, barley, and oats in equal shares, which could have been purchased in 1837, at the then existing prices, by half the annual rent-charge fixed by the Commissioners. In short, the Commissioners fixed the value of the tithes in so much corn in each parish, and the present half-yearly payment is the value at present prices of that quantity of corn. Hence the tithe-owner's income will no longer be affected by increased or diminished fertility; the charge has been fixed once for all; but it will nevertheless increase as the price of corn increases, and diminish as it declines.[2]

It will be seen that this statute, important as it is, makes no change either in the subject titheable or in the destination of ecclesiastical revenues. It preserves the exemptions of lands formerly the property of the religious houses and of glebe, and it expressly provides that any

[1] Official prices are to be published in the *London Gazette* twice a year, and each half-yearly payment is to be made upon the basis of the last declared prices.

[2] The Tithe Commutation Acts do not include personal tithes, and, accordingly, they were not commuted by the Commissioners. It should also be mentioned that, with regard to lands coming under hop or garden cultivation, provision was made by the Acts for the future fixing of an 'extraordinary rent-charge' in addition to the ordinary charge for tithe. These provisions, in consequence of which, as soon as land was cultivated for the above-mentioned purposes, it became subject to a heavy burden, have caused much dissatisfaction, as tending to check the profitable employment of land. See Report of Select Committee of House of Commons, 1881.

right to the rent-charge shall be subject to all the same liabilities to which the right to tithes was formerly subject. In case of non-payment this rent-charge may be distrained for by the owner, who is further empowered, after a certain time, in case of insufficient distress being found on the premises, to take the lands in execution, and keep possession of them till his claim is satisfied.

It may be mentioned that the tithe system grew up in Scotland in Roman Catholic times, as it did in England, and was fully authorised by Parliament. The Teinds, as they are there called, were parsonage or vicarage teinds, corresponding to the great and small tithes, and were payable in kind. At the Reformation parsons and vicars ceased to exist, but the teinds, or what remained of them, were rendered liable to the charge of supporting the minister of the parish, a charge which they still bear. Under Charles I. a commission was appointed to value the teinds, which, by Act of Parliament, were to be taken at one-fifth of the rental. Thus the value of the teinds of a parish depends to a great extent upon whether the valuation was made when land was of small value, or in more recent times. The whole of the teinds, however, are not, any more than the tithes in England, the property of the Church. The Crown, or other *titular* corresponding to the lay impropriator or lay rector in England, absorbed the larger portion of the wealth of the Church. The minister is paid by a stipend upon the tiends. Where the whole tiends have not been already exhausted, they remain subject to a claim by the minister (which is not allowed oftener than once in twenty years) to the augmentation of his stipend out of the 'unexhausted teinds;'

i.e., in fact, out of the rents hitherto received by the heritors (the owners of land) in the parish. It is the business of a division of the Court of Session, known as the Teind Court, to consider and decide upon such applications for augmentation, and to allocate the proper proportion of the stipend upon the different heritors of the parish. There is, therefore, this distinction between English tithes and Scotch teinds: that the rent-charge which now represents the former is a property actually set apart and belonging to its owner, whether ecclesiastical or lay, and is altogether beyond the control of those who have to pay it, viz. *the occupiers* of the land. In Scotland, however, the minister has in many parishes an inchoate right to claim from the *owners* of parochial land a contribution from its profits, which up to the time of the decision of the augmentation suit they had a right to consider their own. The extreme complexity and expense of the proceedings necessary to the prosecution of an augmentation suit, and the uncertainty of the locality (i.e. apportionment) of stipend by the court upon the different heritors, have lately attracted notice, but the efforts hitherto made to remedy a discreditable condition of the law have so far been unavailing.[1]

In England by special custom the clergyman of the parish is often further entitled to the payment of certain offerings and fees, such as Easter dues and surplice fees, or to a fixed sum in lieu of them.

Reasons have been given for the belief that the wealth

---

[1] *Papers on Teinds and Fiars Prices*, by Mr. Nenion Elliot, S.S.C. A Bill for the purpose of simplifying the law was introduced by the Government last session, but was withdrawn.

of the Church has grown enormously with the progress of the nation. Till 1832 no official estimate was ever made of the ecclesiastical revenues or of their expenditure, but in that year a Royal Commission was appointed to enquire into the revenues and patronage of the Church of England and Wales. In 1835 their first report was published, and in that and the succeeding reports a thorough examination was made into the position of the Establishment, and many suggestions were put forward for the consideration of Parliament, a large number of which were subsequently given effect to. The previous unofficial calculations of the income of the Church must have been far within the mark. The Bishop of Landaff, quoted by Dr. Cove, put the *whole* revenues of the Church in 1780 from all sources, including the incomes of the Bishops and other ecclesiastical dignitaries and of the parochial clergy, and even the revenues of the Universities of Oxford and Cambridge and their respective colleges, at one and a half millions. Dr. Cove himself, thirty or forty years later, estimates the income of the beneficed clergy alone, then occupying about ten thousand rectories and vicarages, at two and a half millions, the gross revenue of the bishops at 130,000*l.*, and that of the cathedral and collegiate churches at 275,000*l.* The revenues of the Church were calculated by the Royal Commissioners above referred to on the basis of a three years' average ending on December 31, 1831; a period of years manifestly far too short to give a certain average where much of the income was derived from fines on renewals of leases for lives and for long terms of years. The gross annual income of the two archbishops and twenty-five bishops, then constituting the episcopate, was estimated at 181,600*l*., and the *net* income, after allowing for expenses of collection, salaries of officers, rates and taxes, &c., was put at 160,300*l*. The revenues of the cathedral establishments derived in the main from rents, tithe rent-charges, fines, profits of land, of woods, quarries, and mines, were similarly investigated, and were found to amount, exclusive of Bangor and Sodor and Man, which were without endowed chapters, to a gross annual income of 217,000*l*., or a net annual income of 158,000*l*., to which should be added the large revenues of the establishments of the Collegiate Church of St. Peter's, Westminster (Westminster Abbey), and of St. George's Chapel, Windsor; each of which, though without a bishop, possessed a complete chapter, the latter, indeed, being more richly endowed than any cathedral with the exception of Durham.

At the same date the net income of the beneficed clergy, numbering about 10,700, was estimated at 3,055,000*l*., without taking into account the pay of assistant curates. So much for the revenues of the Church as estimated by Dr. Cove in 1816, and by the Church Commissioners in 1831. So many changes have been made in the last half-century in the organisation of ecclesiastical corporations, and in the distribution of Church revenues, that it is difficult to compare with accuracy the relative financial condition of affairs then and now. The Ecclesiastical Commissioners have become the treasurers, and to some extent the governors, of the Establishment; and the changes that have taken place in consequence will have to be explained later in this work. According to an estimate made in the year 1877—

The incomes of the two archbishops and
28 [1] bishops amount to . . . £163,000
The incomes of 27 chapters to . . . £123,000
„ the parochial clergy, then taken
at 13,300, to £4,277,000

without taking into account the value of the episcopal palaces, or the residences of cathedral dignitaries or of the parochial clergy.[2]

It would, however, be a great mistake to attribute the growth of Church revenues merely to the increased value of Church lands and of the tithe rent-charge. Other assistance on a large scale has been given. In particular, efforts have been made to increase the value of the poorer livings by the establishment of an endowment known as Queen Anne's Bounty, by Parliamentary grants and by voluntary contributions; all of which in modern times have added greatly to the revenues derived from the original ecclesiastical provisions of lands and tithes.

The great poverty of the country clergy for a century and a half after the Reformation has already been noticed. It was not till the rise in the value of land in the eighteenth century that any very real improvement took place. In the time of Queen Anne it was reckoned that six thousand livings were of no greater value than 50*l.* a year, and hundreds were worth less than 20*l.* a year. It

---

[1] This was before the bishopric of Liverpool was founded.

[2] These are the estimates given by Mr. Martin in his very careful work on the *Property and Revenues of the Church of England*. They are based in the main on official returns, on calculations based on the clergy lists, and on a statement submitted by Canon Ashwell to the House of Commons Committee on Public Worship Regulation Bill, 1875.

was, therefore, determined by the Queen, upon the advice of Bishop Burnet, to give up in perpetuity her revenues in firstfruits and tenths, amounting to about 17,000*l.* a year, for the augmentation and maintenance of the poor clergy. These revenues had been, before the Reformation, drawn from the English clergy by the Pope, and had once amounted to a much larger sum. Henry VIII. annexed these by statute to the Crown, which he regarded in this, as in so many other matters, as the lawful heir to the Holy See. Thus it has come to pass that a revenue originally extorted from the clerical estate by the Papal legate Pandulph, in the time of King John, and to the payment of which much parliamentary opposition had been shown, was again to be used for the benefit of the national clergy.

The Statute 2 and 3 Anne, c. 11, gave effect to the good intentions of the Queen. A corporate body, still existing, known as the 'Governors of Queen Anne's Bounty,' was formed, which, after getting rid of certain pensions and charges with which the royal revenues were burdened, proceeded, in the year 1713, to dispose of the annual balance for the purposes intended. From that time to the present day augmentations of the poorer livings[1] have been continuously made out of the funds at the disposal of the governors, which have been largely added to by private benefactions and by parliamentary grants.

The former were called forth by the action of the governors in meeting with the sum of 200*l.* from their

---

[1] The governors were in the first instance to apply the funds in augmenting livings of less than 10*l.* a year.

fund an equal amount voluntarily bestowed. Legal restrictions were removed, so as to enable a donor or testator to devote land or other property for the purpose of improving the condition of the poor clergy, by assigning it to the governors, who were to give effect to the special directions of the benefactor, or, failing such directions, to apply it in the same manner as the rest of their fund. By the year 1825 the private benefactions received by the governors had amounted to 850,000*l.*, and in the following half-century to about 400,000*l.* more.

In 1809 the House of Commons voted the sum of 100,000*l.* to be added to the funds of the corporation, and this grant was continued annually till 1,100,000*l.* had been contributed from the national exchequer. On the whole, it may be taken that the receipts of the Governors of Queen Anne's Bounty, from all sources since its establishment, considerably exceed four millions of money.

CHAPTER VIII.

THE CHURCH BUILDING COMMISSION AND THE ECCLESIASTICAL COMMISSIONERS.

HITHERTO mention has been made of ecclesiastical revenues or income, but the Church is, of course, also in possession of property, largely added to by private generosity and by national expenditure, which is not taken account of in any estimate of annual profit. It would be absurd and impossible to put a money value on the cathedrals, churches, and chapels of the Established Church. At the same time it would be to give a very false notion of the position of the Church towards the State, to omit all mention of the sources from which, as regards its edifices, the Church of England finds itself so magnificently endowed.

In the main the wealth of the Church in this respect was inherited, or rather acquired, at the time of the Reformation, from the Roman Catholics who had created it. The Roman Catholics and the English nation had been formerly one and the same. When the nation, for the most part, ceased to be Catholic, these edifices, like other endowments devoted to the religious instruction of the people, became the property of the Protestant Church of England as by law established. Since then many millions have been spent in repairing, in enlarging, and in adding to the number of national churches; the funds having been provided from ecclesiastical revenues, or by private benefactions, or have been raised by Acts of Parliament. After the Great Fire of London the Legislature imposed a rate for the purpose of rebuilding and restoring the churches of the metropolis, a tax on coals being considered of all 'ways and means' the most suitable for providing money for that great work, the re-erection of St. Paul's Cathedral. In more modern times, when it has been thought needful, the assistance of Parliament has been given, by a general grant out of the national purse. Reference has already been made to the system started in the year 1818 by the statute which established the Church Building Commission. The policy of this and the subsequent Church Building Acts, and of similar statutes, was to vest in a corporate body authority to rearrange old parish bounds and create new parishes and districts, to ascertain where there was the greatest need of fresh church accommodation, and to lay out such sums as Parliament might vote in supplying the deficiency. In the year 1818 a sum of one million was granted for this purpose. Seven years later, this being found inadequate, it was supplemented by a further grant of half a million.

At the same time voluntary efforts on a large scale were being made with the same object. In the year which saw the rise of the Church Building Commission, an Incorporated Society for Promoting the Building and Repairing of Churches and Chapels was established, which in the fifteen following years had expended nearly 200,000*l*., raised entirely by private subscription; and the expenditure of this sum, chiefly in the enlargement and repairing of existing churches, had occasioned the outlay of at least 900,000*l*. more on the part of those who had received the Society's assistance.[1]

Still, great as were the efforts made, they did not keep pace with the difficulties entailed by the immense growth of the population. It will be easily understood that the regular revenues of the Church drawn from the sources enumerated in the last chapter would, from the changed circumstances and condition of the nation in modern times, be often of least avail where they were most required. The enormous increase of the population, and its tendency to collect in the large towns, had produced a state of things with which the Establishment was quite unable to cope. It was not that the resources of the Church were small, but that they were badly applied. It was impossible to make the superabundance of means existing in one place supply the deficiency existing in another. It was the same throughout the whole ecclesiastical organisation. The inequality of the endowments of the various sees, the extensive provisions made for the establishments of cathedrals and collegiate churches, the wealth enjoyed by the incumbent of a parish where there was nothing to do, while in the next parish there was practically no provision at all to meet the religious wants of a large population—these and many other defects of the ecclesiastical system had long attracted attention, and at length called loudly for a remedy.

[1] Second Report of Church Commission, March 1836.

The real state of affairs was not fully known till the reports of the Royal Commission appointed by William IV. were made public. The income of the Episcopate was found sufficient to provide, on an average, 6,000*l.* a year to each see. But how was this distributed? So as to give over 19,000*l.* a year apiece to the Archbishop of Canterbury and the Bishop of Durham; over 11,000*l.* a year to the Archbishop of York, and to each of the Bishops of London, Winchester, and Ely; while Rochester had to put up with less than 1,500*l.*, and Landaff with but 900*l.* a year. The revenues of the cathedrals and collegiate churches were on such a scale that the Commissioners had no hesitation in reporting that the objects of those institutions might be fully secured and continued, and their efficiency maintained, consistently with a considerable reduction of their revenues, a portion of which should be appropriated towards making a better provision for the cure of souls. The deficiency of church accommodation in the big towns, and the dearth of clergy, caused almost a denial of religious instruction to the population of many parishes, so far at least as the State Church was concerned. In four parishes of London and the suburbs, containing over 160,000 persons, there was church accommodation for little over 8,000, while in the same district there were but eleven clergymen; and this notwithstanding that so much had been done by private generosity and by Act of Parliament to increase the number of churches and chapels and to augment benefices throughout the kingdom. In many parishes the income was too small to support a clergyman, so that the work was often done by the incumbent of another parish, thus giving rise to another evil, that of non-residence and the holding of a plurality of livings by one clergyman. Nearly 300 livings were found to be of less value than 50*l.* a year, rather more than 2,000 less than 100*l.*, and about 3,500 less than 150*l.*, and in many of these incumbencies there was no house for the incumbent. At the other end of the scale were nearly 200 livings enjoying an income exceeding 1,000*l.* a year, the most valuable being that of Doddington, in the diocese of Ely, where, owing to the reclamation of fen land, the tithe had enormously increased. The net income of this benefice was put by the Commissioners at over 7,000*l.* a year, while a living in the diocese of Durham was put at nearly 5,000*l.* To remedy such a state of things, many important recommendations were made. The episcopate was not to be increased, the creation recommended of the two new sees of Manchester and Ripon being counterbalanced by the union recommended of Bristol and Llandaff and of Bangor and St. Asaph. And in many cases the boundaries of the dioceses were to be varied, so as to make a fairer division of episcopal superintendence and labour. The incomes of the bishops were to be equalised after reserving a higher pay for the archbishops and more dignified sees, and a method of doing this was suggested. Cathedral establishments were to be reduced; and the creation of a perpetual body was recommended, which should receive from sees and cathedrals the excess of revenue beyond their fixed requirements, should apply these funds in a specified way, and should carry into execution the changes required.

In the main the recommendations of the Commissioners were carried out, though as to some of the details the Commissioners themselves changed their opinions, as in advising the union, which ultimately took place, of the sees of Bristol and Gloucester, instead of Bristol and Llandaff as first proposed. The sees of Bangor and St. Asaph were ultimately kept separate, and the bishopric of Sodor and Man, which it had been intended to add to the diocese of Carlisle, was after all preserved as a distinct diocese out of deference to the dissatisfaction expressed by the Manxmen at the idea of losing their bishop. The recommendation of the Church Commission, however, which in importance outweighed all the others, was given effect to at once; viz. that which advised the creation of a permanent body in whose hands surplus Church revenues should be allowed to accumulate, so as to form a fund out of which payments for specified purposes might be made. By the Statute 6 and 7 William IV. c. 77 a perpetual corporation with a common seal was constituted, under the name of the Ecclesiastical Commissioners, and to their body as subsequently modified have been given from time to time more and more extensive powers, till it has become in reality for many purposes the executive authority of the Established Church. The original composition of this corporation under the Act of 1836 seemed almost to contemplate its becoming a department of the State, so closely were its members connected with the Government of the day. The First Lord of the Treasury, the Lord Chancellor, a Secretary of State, the Lord President of the Council, and the Chancellor of the Exchequer, with the Archbishops and the Bishops of London, Lincoln, and Gloucester, with three distinguished laymen named in the Act, formed the original Ecclesiastical Commission, and provision was made that in supplying vacancies the proportion of laymen to bishops should be preserved, and that the former should of necessity be members of the Church of England. Four years later, however,[1] a great change was made in the composition of the Commission, *all* the bishops being added to it, the two Chief Justices, the Chief Baron, the Master of the Rolls, and the Judge of the Admiralty Court, the Deans of Canterbury, Westminster, and St. Paul's, and four laymen, of whom two were to be appointed by the Crown and two by the Archbishop of Canterbury, security as before being taken for the churchmanship of the lay members. In the year 1850 the Queen was empowered to add two laymen, and the Archbishop of Canterbury one,[2] to the Ecclesiastical Commission, whose special business it should be as Church Estates Commissioners to consider and conduct, on behalf of the Ecclesiastical Commissioners, all matters having reference to the sale, the leasing, the exchange, and the general management of lands. The effect of these changes was not merely to create a preponderance of the spiritual over the lay element in the Commission, but to withdraw the general management of business from the latter, of whom a large proportion rarely or never attended its meetings.[3]

---

[1] See 3 and 4 Vict. c. 113.

[2] The first Estates Commissioner receives a salary of 1,200*l.* a year, and the Archbishop's Commissioner a salary of 1,000*l.* a year, while the second Commissioner is unpaid.

[3] See the effect of these changes in the constitution of the Commission, examined by Mr. Martin, *Property and Revenues of English Church,* p. 118 *et seq.*

The necessity of dealing with the Church revenues as a whole has been pointed out, if its great resources were to be made the most of. But, at the same time, nothing could be less in accordance with the fundamental principles of the English Establishment than the creation of a perpetual corporation to hold as trustee for the Church at large a fund derived from the different and independent ecclesiastical estates of which that Church was composed. No wonder that such a change, however beneficial in itself, should excite the fears of the timid, some of whom almost attributed to the Spiritual Commissioners treachery to the Church, whose best interests they were in truth serving. The great principle of the inviolability of the Established Church, so it was said, had been given up; the principle, namely, that the Church as a corporation possesses *no property* which is applicable to general purposes, but that each particular ecclesiastical corporation, whether aggregate or sole, has its property separate, distinct, and inalienable. 'The wealthier endowments of our ecclesiastical corporations aggregate, the reward and dignified ease of many who had spent their lives in the arduous discharge of the duties of their profession, and the inducements alike to the higher ranks of society and to brighter talents to undertake those duties, and which had rendered the body of our clergy so superior to those of other countries, were overthrown and ruined without a struggle. . . The regrets, however, came too late . . . . and the Church could not complain of a spoliation' which its own members did not courageously resist, and so forth.[1] Fortunately these regrets *were* too late; and the nation

[1] Cripps, *Laws of the Church and the Clergy.*

in general, and the members of the Church of England in particular, have great reason to be thankful for the bold criticisms and the decided policy of the Church and Ecclesiastical Commissions.

It would be far beyond the limits of such a work as the present to give in any detail an account of the operations of the Ecclesiastical Commissioners. They dealt, to begin with, with the episcopal revenues, estimating the value of the estates of each, and requiring, on the happening of a vacancy, that the new bishop should pay over the whole episcopal income after deducting the annual sum fixed upon as a sufficient endowment for that see. The Commissioners thus became, by the receipt of revenues from the richer sees, possessed of a considerable fund, called the Episcopal Fund, out of which they were able to augment the poorer bishoprics. By a change of system in 1860, however, the Commissioners, on a vacancy occurring, were to become possessed of all the estates of the vacant see, and were then to assign lands sufficient to produce the statutory revenue required. A similar policy was followed with respect to the capitular estates, it being the intention that the incomes of the dignitaries of the Church should be on the statutory scale, and should be derived from landed estates reannexed by the Commissioners to each bishop and each dean and chapter. The income derived from the cathedral estates by the Ecclesiastical Commissioners far exceeded the revenues the cathedrals had received from the same lands; and as the advice of the Commissioners greatly to reduce cathedral establishments was followed by the Legislature, the former soon found themselves in possession of a large fund, called the Common Fund, out of which the general objects aimed at were to be provided.

The net income of the estates of the see of Canterbury (to take an example), in 1851, was about 24,000*l.*; and the statutory emoluments of the Archbishop having been fixed at 15,000*l.*, the Commissioners thus received a revenue of 9,000*l.* per annum. But the receipts derived by the Commissioners from their better management of the capitular estates, and from the reduction of cathedral establishments, were far larger than resulted from their operations upon the episcopal revenues, and hence the Common Fund at the disposal of the Commissioners soon became very considerable.

The statutory scale of episcopal income is now for the

Archbishop of Canterbury	£15,000	per annum.
„ York	10,000	„
Bishop of London	10,000	„
„ Durham	8,000	„
„ Winchester	6,500	„

while the average income of the remainder of the bishops is between 4,000*l.* and 5,000*l.*

The regular establishment of a cathedral in modern times now consists of a dean and four canons, though there are several where a larger number of canons is allowed. In the different establishments the incomes of the dignitaries differ considerably, one dean enjoying 3,000*l.* a year and several over 2,000*l.*, while the average income of the whole number of deans is about 1,500*l.* and that of the canons about 750*l.* After the rearrangements of the episcopal incomes had been completed, there was still a balance remaining. This was added to the Common Fund, with which in the year 1851 the Episcopal Fund was merged. From time to time greater authority has been given to the Ecclesiastical Commissioners. Thus in 1856 they acquired the extensive powers of the Church Building Commissioners, above referred to. It is their function to endow churches, to create districts, to augment livings, and to manage landed estates the whole rental of which exceeds 850,000*l.* per annum.

In their last report [1] they glance at the position and prospects of the Common Fund, and at the work they have accomplished in the forty years elapsed since its establishment.

They tell us of nearly five thousand benefices augmented and endowed, partly in annual payments, partly in lands, and partly in improvement of parsonage-houses, these augmentations amounting to 'about 620,000*l.* per annum;' and they tell us of another sum of 145,000*l.* a year, received from private benefactors and administered by them for the same purpose. Thus the total increase in the incomes of benefices made through the instrumentality of the Commissioners amounts to 765,000*l.*, or to such an income as would be derived from a capital sum of about 23,000,000*l.*

To sum up the position of the Church towards its endowments, we find large property held by the bishops, by the cathedrals, and by the parochial clergy; while the new corporation of the Ecclesiastical Commissioners also holds very large endowments in land and money, to be applied in the manner directed by Parliament. What

[1] 33rd *Report of the Ecclesiastical Commissioners*, 1881.

the total income of the Church may be, as drawn from these various sources, it is less easy to calculate than the amount directly *expended* in the remuneration of the established clergy. We find the actual income of the whole episcopate, and of the deans and chapters, to be under 300,000*l.* a year, while the income of the parochial clergy, as we have already seen, may be taken at 4,270,000*l.*, and this estimate is exclusive of the value of the episcopal, cathedral, and parochial residences occupied by the clergy.

CHAPTER IX.

APPOINTMENT OF DIGNITARIES AND PATRONAGE.

WITHOUT, it is hoped, going into greater detail than was necessary, some idea has been given in the last two chapters of the wealth of the Established Church, and the sources whence it is drawn. There is much said in the present day of the poverty and of the hardships of the clergy; and with nearly 1,200 livings of less than 100*l.* a year, it is evident that the parochial provision is often quite inadequate for the support in an independent position of a parish minister of the attainments and calibre desired. If he does his duty efficiently, he will have but little time, even if he possesses the primary qualifications, to better, by his own exertions in other directions, his pecuniary position. When Warrington and his friend Arthur Pendennis found but few clients willing to clamber up the three pairs of stairs to their chambers in the Temple, they had no difficulty in discovering another market for their wares. They lived to a great extent, as so many of the junior and poorer members of their profession have done, by the pen. When, on the other hand, the Vicar of Hogglestock, on the 130*l.* per annum of his Cornish living, had to encounter the penury and disease which were afflicting his household, neither his scholarship, which as his only wealth he endeavoured to share among his children, nor his pride, diminished his or their sufferings, or enabled him the better to succeed in the 'struggle for existence.'[1] In comparing the remuneration of different professions or trades, account must be taken of the very different conditions under which they are practised. As regards remuneration, officers of the army after twenty years' service are possibly in no better position than that *at once* attained by their old schoolfellows who on leaving college had entered the ranks of the clergy. Had the above-mentioned vicar instead of the Church selected the army as his career, he would have been earning as Lieutenant Crawley for many years from 120*l*. to 140*l*. per annum, and as Captain Crawley but little over 200*l*., which after providing himself with uniform and other necessaries, would have left less than nothing for Mrs. Crawley and the children. In all probability the Captain, unless a man of private means, would have remained a bachelor; but this prudent course, even if to the taste of the clergyman himself, is not one which in a Protestant country public feeling would approve the clergy in general pursuing. The country requires a married clergy; and in this respect it must be confessed that the clergy show no unwillingness to respond to the expectations formed of them. All must agree that the low scale of payment in many livings is absolutely discreditable to the Church; yet it cannot be said that upon the whole, taking one profession with another, the clergy are ill-paid. It would be a

---

[1] Trollope's *Framley Parsonage*.

doubtful benefit to the nation and to the Church itself that those who enter the ranks of the clergy should be influenced in the main by the desire to obtain some lucrative office or rich benefice; and a low scale of reward, if it tends on the one hand to make the ministry attractive *as a mere profession* only to the very poor, may be expected to tend on the other to exclude those of higher position and greater means *unless* they are acting under the influence of higher motives than those of pecuniary profit.[1] Still, it would be a mistake against which all history, ecclesiastical and lay, warns us, to suppose that the clergy as a body (however much individual clergymen may rise superior to selfish instincts) are less acted upon by worldly considerations and ambitious motives than other classes of men; and it may therefore be useful to notice some of the professional advantages which the career of a clergyman presents; and this without intending

---

[1] In connection with this subject it would not be fair to omit all mention of *the assistant curates*, who are sometimes most wretchedly remunerated for very hard and most useful work. Still, on entering the Church the young curate cannot be worse remunerated than 'unpaid *attachés*,' most barristers, and young officers in the army, since it is only under exceptional circumstances that in any of these professions *any* profit can for some time be earned. As regards the curates, there is some reason to believe that, on the average, they are no worse off than the poorer incumbents.

It is said that the pay of 5,000 curates is probably equal to that of any 5,000 incumbents that could be chosen. (See letter to the *Times* of February 4, 1882, from 'An Incumbent,' based on the statistics of the *Financial Reformer's Almanac*.) Of course in the profession of clergymen, as in other professions, there are numerous 'failures' to be lamented.

See also provisions in favour of assistant curates contained in 1 & 2 Vict. c. 106.

to suggest that in the wealthy Church of England more than in other churches is there to be found a superfluity of those—

> Who, for their bellies' sake,
> Creep, and intrude, and climb into the fold.[1]

In the last chapter, reference was made to a complaint that the clergyman's position was ceasing to be attractive to men of the higher and more cultivated classes of society, in consequence of the diminution of those rewards to which formerly so many of them were enabled to look forward. At the present day, with thirty-two bishoprics, to twenty-six of which life peerages are attached, with some thirty deaneries, and with one hundred and thirty-four canonries, with a dozen livings of over 2,000$l.$ a year, and with many more of over 1,000$l.$, it can hardly be said that the prizes of the profession are either too few or too poor. But when it is recollected that other places of considerable emolument, and of very great dignity, are almost monopolised by the clergy—such, for instance, as the head masterships of the large public schools, and the headships of the colleges of Oxford and Cambridge—it may be doubted whether in any profession the generality of its members have a better chance of reaching an enviable position than have the clergy of the Church of England. It is true that very many livings are wretchedly poor, but there are some two thousand worth more than 500$l.$ a year; and it is the common experience of everyone that throughout the length and breadth of England, if the stranger observes a more than usually commodious, snug, and unpretending-looking little country house, with its gardens and grounds

[1] Milton: *Lycidas*.

neatly kept, affording every indication of modest comfort, the chances are, that on inquiry he will find that the fortunate owner is the parish clergyman.

It is now time to explain the system by which appointments of church dignitaries are made, and the way in which, and the persons by whom, clergymen are selected to fill incumbencies.

To begin with the bishops, it seems that they were in early times throughout the whole of Christendom elected to their sees, laity as well as clergy taking part in the election. Afterwards the right of election was confined to the clergy, and it has already been noticed how the very first clause of Magna Charta reserved to the monasteries and cathedrals the right freely to elect their abbots and bishops. The king was not to refuse his assent to their choice without reasonable and lawful cause. The election of the bishop by the dean and chapter was thus the regular practice in England, and so continued after the Reformation, except during the reign of Edward VI., who was enabled by Parliament to dispense altogether with such election, and to appoint by royal letters patent. Ever since Edward VI.'s reign, however, this election has been a mere form, the appointment being virtually made by the Crown. Upon the occurring of a vacancy in any see a *congé d'élire*, or permission to proceed to an election, is despatched to the dean and chapter by the sovereign; but this is accompanied by royal letters missive, in which is designated the person whom the chapter is to elect. In case of the chapter refusing to elect, it will, under 25 Henry VIII. c. 20, incur the penalties of a præmunire, and after the lapse of a certain number of days the Crown may appoint by letters patent. As regards the late Irish Establishment, bishops were appointed at once by letters patent; and the appointments to the new English sees, such as Truro, St. Albans, Liverpool, &c., where there are as yet no chapters in existence, are made in the same fashion.

In the first session of the present Parliament a Bill was introduced [1] into the House of Commons for the purpose of abolishing the system of *congé d'élire*, and of giving to the Crown the power to appoint to all bishoprics by letters patent. It was rejected by a small majority upon the second reading after a short and interesting debate, in which it was strongly urged that the retention of the mere form of election, connected as it is with a religious ceremony, is, if not absolutely irreverent, but little better than a delusion and a sham, and that of all methods of appointment, that by the Crown upon the advice of the Prime Minister duly responsible to Parliament is the best that can be found. On the other hand, it was contended by several members that the form should be retained, in the hope that in time the election would become a reality—an expectation which it is safe to predict will never be verified so long as the connection between Church and State is maintained.

When the bishop has been appointed in the manner specified, he receives consecration at the hands of the archbishop and two other bishops; the presence of three bishops being necessary for the due transmission of the Episcopal authority in its spiritual aspect to the bishop elect. The form of service to be used on these occasions

[1] By Mr. Monk, June 1, 1880. Rejected by 97 to 72.

is contained in the Prayer-book, and is therefore sanctioned by the Act of Uniformity.

In former times deans were, like bishops, elected by the chapters in pursuance of a *congé d'élire* from the Crown, accompanied with letters missive of recommendation; but the independent action of the chapters in such a case did not, as in Episcopal elections, render them liable to a præmunire; and as regards all deaneries in England in the present day, whether of cathedrals or collegiate churches, the appointment is made by the Crown by letters patent without any election at all.

The appointment to canonries is made either by the Crown, by the bishops, by the Lord Chancellor, or by the universities, the patronage of by far the larger number being vested either in the bishops or in the Crown. To whomsoever the patronage of these high ecclesiastical dignities is given, it is to be exercised with a regard to the interests of the public and of the Church, and not to be made use of as a means of private gain by the patron, who, as we have seen, is either a member of the Government, and as such responsible to Parliament, or a high officer of the Church, whose position renders his action matter of public interest and observation.

It would hardly have been necessary to notice as a characteristic of the ecclesiastical patronage just mentioned that its possession is treated as a public trust rather than as private property, were it not that unfortunately a very different and extraordinary state of things exists with regard to other very valuable patronage of the Establishment, to which it is now time to turn our attention. We have already seen that the total income of the beneficed clergy exceeds 4,000,000*l*. a year. Thus both from the largeness of the pecuniary interests involved, and the importance of the duties the parochial clergy have to perform, the right of appointing to benefices, and the way in which the right is exercised, are matters of great public interest. This right of patronage, as it is called, has never in England been exercised by the parishioners themselves, except in a few instances,[1] nor have they ever set up any claim to control in any way the action of the person who has the right to appoint their spiritual teacher. A claim to veto the appointment of an unfit presentee, a protest against the 'intrusion' into the parish of an obnoxious pastor, such as have roused in Scotland the strongest feelings of the people, have never disturbed the rights which the law of England recognises in the owner of patronage. This absence of all wish on the part of the people to have any voice in the selection of the parish minister, who exists for their benefit, and whose character and qualifications are to them of the highest importance, it is difficult to understand; unless indeed they are willing to accept the humble position of a flock towards its pastor even in such a matter as this, not caring for a change in the law which, as the Scotch poet says,—

> Would give the brutes the power themselves
> To choose their herds.'

Whatever the reason, there is no popular check in England upon the rights of patrons, and but little legal

[1] As for instance in the case of the perpetual curacy of Clerkenwell.

security taken that the right should be even decently exercised.

In times immediately before the Reformation lay patronage was practically unknown,[1] appointments to the cure of souls being made by the ecclesiastical corporations, bishops, deans and chapters or religious houses; but upon the large transfer of property from ecclesiastical to lay owners under Henry VIII., much of this patronage also changed hands, and at the present day the patronage of about half of the benefices of the kingdom belongs to private individuals. The patronage of the rest is in the hands of the Crown, the Lord Chancellor, the bishops, the cathedral authorities, the universities, and their colleges. Of these the bishops and cathedral authorities own by far the largest share.

Before referring to the way in which the patrons exercise their rights, the right itself must be explained. What is patronage? It is the right of appointing to a benefice having the cure of souls, on the occurrence of a vacancy. This right may be unlimited; *i.e.*, it may be a right to appoint whensoever and as often as a vacancy may

---

[1] This appears to be the correct view, speaking generally, of the parochial incumbencies. No doubt there were some cases where, in consequence of having handsomely endowed a church, the lay benefactor claimed the patronage. On the other hand, the view taken by most legal writers, including Blackstone and Sir Robert Phillimore, is that even with regard to the original parochial divisions, lay patronage dates from the earliest times. The account given in the text, however, seems more consistent with the theory held among Roman Catholics about gifts made to the Church. And Mr. Martin says there can be no doubt of its correctness. (See *Properties and Revenues of the Church of England*.)

occur; or it may be confined to a right to appoint to the benefice when it *next* falls vacant.

This former right of patronage is called an advowson, while the latter one is known as a right of next presentation. Certain distinctions are made between these, but both advowsons and next presentations are treated as property, and as such may be sold, or mortgaged, or left by will, or in case of intestacy will descend to the heir-at-law of the deceased. There are some owners of advowsons who, while having a full right of property, so as to be able to transfer them to others, are yet *themselves* not permitted by the law to appoint to the benefice, should it become vacant. Thus if the patron be a Roman Catholic or a foreigner, in the first case the presentation would be made by one of the universities, in the latter case by the Crown. But should the patron be a Jew, he would be as fully entitled to present to the vacant benefice as if he were Archbishop of Canterbury.[1]

The general law of the Church considers the corrupt presentation of a clergyman to a benefice, in return for money or reward, a grievous sin and heresy. The Statute Law of England, and the Common Law also, subject to penalties the perpetrators of such nefarious transactions. The conduct of Simon the sorcerer, visited with the severest condemnation by St. Peter, has remained throughout the whole history of Christianity and among all its branches a warning for those who would purchase for

---

[1] But should a Jew hold an office under the Crown to which belongs a right of patronage, the right is to devolve upon the Archbishop of Canterbury for the time being. 21 & 22 Vict. c. 49.

money spiritual powers, thereby becoming guilty of the crime of 'Simony.' Every clergyman, on being presented to a living by the patron, has to make the declaration against simony of which mention has already been made (ante, p. 58). Nevertheless the only check upon the free traffic in livings in the English Church, is that a *clergyman* is not permitted to buy a next presentation, and that no one is permitted to sell a living which is actually vacant.[1] A clergyman may buy an advowson and present himself as soon as the vacancy occurs, and may if he likes afterwards sell the advowson. A patron may sell an advowson or next presentation when the present incumbent is tottering to his grave, the prospect of 'immediate possession' of course greatly enhancing the price. This traffic in livings is not necessarily carried on in the dark, nor is it only occasionally resorted to here and there by a shameless patron or priest. On the contrary it is systematic, and carried on in the face of day. The 'Ecclesiastical Gazette,' a monthly journal sent to every clergyman whose name appears in the *Clergy List*, contains *advertisements* of livings to the number of perhaps eighty or a hundred per month. The cure of souls is frequently at a public auction knocked down to the highest bidder. The agency in livings is as recognised a business as is house agency in London. It has been calculated that there are perhaps two thousand livings of the Church on sale, some by public auction, but far the greater number by private contract. The advantages testified to by the

---

[1] The advowson might be sold, but the next presentation would not pass by the sale.

advertisers, are generally such as high pay and little work, picturesque neighbourhood and good society, opportunities for indulging sporting tastes, and so forth; while of course the prospect of 'immediate possession' turning on the age or infirmity of the existing incumbent is the element of most importance in the bargain. The presentee may be unfit, but the law regards as sacred the private rights of property of the patron, and is not easily enlisted in the interests of the parishioners. Hence the bishop has generally as a matter of fact no power to refuse admission to any clergyman duly presented by the patron. It is needless to observe that scandals such as these have called forth the condemnation of the bishops, and of many distinguished churchmen, yet it is astonishing that the general feeling of members, lay or ecclesiastical, of the Church of England in an age when the sale of pocket boroughs is looked back upon as a sign of the defective morality of our ancestors, and when the sale and purchase of promotion in the army shocked the public sense of right as much as it interfered with the welfare of the service, should tolerate with equanimity such a disgraceful practice, or should leave for a single year unchanged the laws which permit it. It is also most remarkable, that notwithstanding the impetus towards reform which has been given by the bishops,[1] the efforts made in the House of Commons to remove this scandal from the Church have been chiefly due to dis-

---

[1] See Report of House of Lords' Committee on Patronage in 1874, of which the Bishop of Peterborough was Chairman. It is impossible to use stronger language than that of some of the Bishops in condemnation of this traffic.

senters.[1] The Lords Committee of 1874, which brought to light many abuses connected with the traffic in livings, nevertheless reported in favour of the maintenance of the system of private patronage, as tending to secure among the parochial clergy a fair representation of the different sections and views of churchmen; a variety essential to the existence of the Establishment, and difficult of attainment in any other way.

With regard to the patronage vested in the colleges of Oxford and Cambridge, the regular practice used to be to fill up the vacancy in a living by appointing the senior fellow of his college without any particular reference to the needs of the parish or the qualifications of the senior fellow; but in these days, though this is still the rule, it is not uncommon to make exceptions to it where it would lead to the appointing of an unfit incumbent.[2]

Under recent statutes which have been passed to meet the want felt by a growing population for new churches and new ecclesiastical districts, and in the efforts to add to the value of poor livings, considerable increase in the amount of private patronage has been brought about. Thus, when a district is created under the new Parishes Acts, the patronage, though to begin with it is vested in the Ecclesiastical Commissioners, is to be assigned to any

---

[1] See the two speeches of Mr. Leatham in the House of Commons, June 26 1877, and February 12, 1878.

[2] See Evidence given to the Lords' Committee, and see also the clever sketch of 'the Rector' in the *Chronicles of Carlingford*, where that worthy but fossilised hero is the victim of the old college system of appointing to a cure of souls in a country parish, for which a quarter of a century of life as a resident fellow in the university had utterly unfitted him.

benefactor who will permanently endow the living with money or land up to a certain proportion of the whole. Again, the Lord Chancellor is empowered by another statute to sell livings of which he is patron, and out of the purchase money to increase the endowment of the living sold, or to add to that of other poor livings in his gift. There is therefore no sign of any growing public dissatisfaction with the system of the appointment of the clergy to their spheres of duty by laymen; but it is to be hoped that means will be discovered to ensure the proper exercise by the latter of the privileges which the law gives them.

CHAPTER X.

'ESTABLISHED' AND 'FREE' CHURCHES.

THE sources whence the Church derives its wealth have been enumerated, and the system upon which its revenues are distributed among the dignitaries, and rank and file, of the clergy has also been described. Let us consider whether there is anything peculiar in the nature of its ownership of property, due to the fact of its being 'the established,' that is the national Church. A large portion of the wealth of the Church is, as we have seen, directly derived from its Roman Catholic predecessor, while another very large portion is derived from the continued application of the tithe principle, no longer in favour of the Roman Catholic, but entirely for the benefit of the Protestant religion as established by law. A third portion of its endowments has been provided out of general taxation, and a fourth by voluntary benefactions. Every church in England, except the Established Church, whether Catholic, Protestant, Greek, or Jew, is supported solely and entirely by voluntary contributions, or the proceeds of former contributions. The Cathedrals of Canterbury, Durham, Salisbury, and Westminster Abbey were not erected by persons professing either a belief in the Thirty-nine Articles, or obedience to the Act of Uniformity. The Roman Catholic looks at these splendid buildings with as much sorrow as admiration, feeling that his religion has been robbed of its grandest monuments, erected on spots hallowed by the miracles or the martyrdom of its saints. The Protestant dissenter may feel, on the other hand, that his own exclusion is somewhat hard when he calls to mind that it was in these buildings that the whole nation for centuries worshipped, whilst, after all, those in whose favour he is excluded are, from the religious standpoint of the old persuasion, fully as much heretics as himself.

In the beginning of his 'History of the Thirty Years' War' Schiller illustrates the difficulty that arises, when a religious community splits into two antagonistic sections, by referring to the difficulties of private inheritance. Where two brothers have shared the possessions they have inherited from their father, and one of them at length determines to leave the paternal home, it becomes necessary to make some division of the inheritance. Their father, since he could not foresee, had not made any provision for the separation of his sons. So, for more than a thousand years the wealth of the Church had been steadily accumulating out of the benefactions of an ancestry, who were quite as much the ancestors of the son who leaves his home, as of the son who stays behind. The endowments had belonged to the Catholic Church, because there was none other in existence; to the eldest son, because he was as yet the only son. But at length the question arises: does the right of primogeniture exist in the Church? Could Lutherans be excluded from sharing in wealth in part created by their ancestors, simply for the reason that at the time of its creation there was no distinction between Lutherans and Catholics?

So in England, it can hardly be maintained that the nation, on becoming in the main Protestant, was not justly entitled to employ for its religious purposes in a different form the resources it had previously devoted to the maintenance of the only form of religion then known to it. And as with the original breach between Catholics and Protestants, so with the more recent separations from the established religion. In each case it is for the State to determine upon the equity and expediency of dividing the inheritance, or of making such fresh arrangements as the welfare of the whole nation in the altered condition of affairs may require. It is supposed by some persons, that the Church of England rightly asserts a claim to the sole heirship of the old Roman Catholic Church, because it is in spite of all changes *the same church*; this being very different (so it is said) from the relation of the Presbyterian Establishment in Scotland to *its* Roman Catholic predecessor, where there was a breach of continuity which prevents the reformed Scotch Church having an equitable claim to any such inheritance. The true heirs in that country would not be the Church, but rather that body of Episcopalian dissenters who adhere to the purified form of the old religion. All this rests upon the strangest misconception of what constitute the true title-deeds of a State Church.

The fact that the Church of England is Episcopalian and the Church of Scotland Presbyterian gives no better or more equitable claim to the former than to the latter church to enjoy the endowments of the old Roman Catholic religion. It is not by virtue of its holding a special creed: but in consequence of the creed it holds recommending itself to the nation as a whole, that a church can claim the exclusive benefit of national endowments, or the appropriation to itself of a portion of the general taxation. The expression 'national endowments' as applied to the revenues of the Established Church is therefore an accurate one, and serves to point out the great distinction that exists between these and the private property of individuals or of voluntary societies. The cathedral and the parish church are in a sense national institutions quite as much as they are places of worship of a particular denomination of Christians.

The tendency, however, in the present day is for the Church to rely more and more on voluntary effort, and less on State assistance. It may be confidently predicted that Parliament will never make another grant out of the public purse to build fresh churches for the Establishment. Yet it is not found that there is any deficiency of money available for such a purpose. On the contrary, the flow of benefactions is said to be inexhaustible; and in the seventeen years previous to 1875, the sums voluntarily contributed to the building of churches in the newly created ecclesiastical districts amounted to nearly five millions of money. In our own times church rates have been abolished, the money expended upon the repair of ordinary parish churches being now obtained entirely from voluntary contributions. And as with church building and church repairing, so with many other objects of the Church, has it become the tendency to trust to private generosity to supply the requisite funds. We have seen how the efforts of Queen Anne's Bounty board and of the Ecclesiastical Commissioners, to increase the endowment of poorer livings have been seconded by voluntary assistance. Only a few years ago, an entirely voluntary society was started by Lord Lorne with a similar object, viz., to increase the value of small livings up to 200*l*. a year. The Bishop of London's Fund, depending entirely on subscriptions and collections, has received in the eighteen years of its existence over 650,000*l*. for the purpose of building and repairing churches and schools, improving clergymen's houses, providing mission-rooms and scripture readers, and otherwise aiding the parochial work of the metropolis. It would be impossible to mention all the voluntary associations which contribute their assistance to carrying on the work of the Church. It is no exaggeration to say, with the author [1] already so often quoted, that at the present day *the growth* of the Church of England, as shown in the erection of new places of worship, has come to be mainly dependent on voluntary contributions. So with the increase of the Episcopate. Three years ago an Act of Parliament was passed, enabling the Queen by Order in Council, to create four new bishoprics, viz., Liverpool, Newcastle, Wakefield and Southwell, so soon as endowments to the extent of 3,500*l*. per annum should be provided. In the main these were to be obtained by private benefactions, though to some extent they were to be assisted by deductions from the income of other sees, and from other revenues of the Church. The two first of these have been already founded.

[1] Martin, *Revenues of the Church of England.*

It need hardly cause surprise, if, when the Church takes to relying so much on the voluntary contributions of its own members, it should become more impatient of external control. Still it should not be forgotten, that gifts are made by benefactors with their eyes open to a national institution, and the largeness of the contributions may show satisfaction with this character of the Church as often as preference for the special religious characteristics of a particular denomination of Christians. In short, a benefactor, while wishing to devote his property to religious purposes, may prefer to bestow it in a manner where he may reasonably expect that national, rather than sectarian interests will be considered; and for this he may look for some security in the influence exercised by the State over the Church with which it is connected. Thus though in modern times the National Church draws a large revenue from sources exactly similar to those from which Free Churches draw their supplies, yet because the former is the State Church, its property is held subject to the conditions, and to be applied to the purposes which the State prescribes as best conducing to the welfare of the nation; that is, as Lord Palmerston shortly put it, 'the property of the Church belongs to the State.'[1]

To discuss, still less to advocate, political changes in the constitution or connection of Church and State, does not of course come within the object of this work, which is simply to explain the meaning of existing institutions, and the principles apparently involved in them. And it is for this purpose only that reference is now made to the disestablishment of the Church of Ireland. In that

[1] House of Commons' Debates, 1856.

country we have the means of making a comparison between the status of an 'Established' Church, and of the same church when 'Disestablished,' or freed from all connection with the State. It was the object of the Government, and of Parliament in 1869 to sever entirely the connection between the Church and the State in Ireland, and to make the former a voluntary association, on an equal footing with the other Free Churches of the country. How was this done? What changes, in short, did the Irish Church Act of 1869 bring about in the Church of Ireland, to transform it from a State Church into a Free Church? In the first place the ecclesiastical corporations, sole or aggregate, were dissolved; the bishops were to lose their seats in the House of Lords; the Crown was to give up its right of appointing church dignitaries, and its other patronage.[1] Patronage was taken from owners of advowsons, who were duly compensated. Bishops, clergy and laity were empowered to appoint a representative body, which was to be incorporated by Her Majesty as the governing body of the Church. The ecclesiastical courts and the ecclesiastical law were abolished, and all ecclesiastical jurisdiction was to cease. As regards property, the intention was to vest the whole in a temporary commission with full protection for life interests, and instructions to re-endow the church body with the churches, and glebe houses, and with what were called 'private endowments,' *i.e.* all endowments made by private individuals to the church since 1660: whilst due provision was also made for the maintenance of those historic buildings of the church, which as 'national monuments' it

[1] In Ireland the sale of livings, which is such a scandal to the Church of England, was very rare.

was the interest of the country at large should be efficiently maintained.

On January 1, 1871, as Mr. Gladstone in bringing in the Bill stated it, 'the ecclesiastical courts in Ireland would be abolished, the ecclesiastical jurisdiction in Ireland would cease, the ecclesiastical laws in Ireland would no longer bind by any authority of law, the rights of peerage would lapse on the part of the bishops, and all ecclesiastical corporations in that country would be dissolved,' and hence '*disestablishment of the Irish Church would be legally completed.*'

Thus the Irish Church acquired a new constitution; its governing authority being no longer the Parliament of the United Kingdom, but a general Synod consisting at present of two Houses which sit together, viz., the House of Bishops, in which the twelve prelates have seats, and the House of Representatives in which there are two hundred and eight clerical, and four hundred and sixteen lay representatives. And this organisation was created, not by Parliament, but by the members of the Church, and is subject to such alterations as the Synod itself may think it right to make, without being subject to the control of any external authority.

The Act of 1869 effected a great change in the constitution of the Irish Church, and a considerable transfer of property to national purposes other than those to which it had been previously dedicated. The abolition however of the ecclesiastical law, and of the jurisdiction of the ecclesiastical courts must be explained, as its effect might otherwise be supposed to be much greater than was actually the case. Mr. Gladstone, in the speech already referred to, explained, that although the ecclesiastical laws were to lose their force *as laws,* in which respect they bore a relation to the whole community, yet they would continue to exist as a form of *voluntary contract,* which would bind together the bishops, clergy and laity of the church, till they should be duly altered by the new representative governing body, which the members of that church were to appoint. And in accordance with this intention, the Act of 1869 provided 'that the present ecclesiastical laws of Ireland, and the present articles, doctrines, rights, rules, discipline and ordinances of the said church, subject to future alterations, should be binding on members of the church, as if such members had mutually contracted and agreed to abide by and observe the same, and should be *capable of being enforced in the temporal courts* in relation to any property which was reserved by the Act to the church or its members, as if such property had been expressly conveyed in trust, to be held by persons bound to obey the said ecclesiastical laws, articles, doctrines, rights, rules, discipline and ordinances of the said church.'

Thus the Irish Disestablishment Act affected, first the Church Constitution, secondly the Church Laws, and thirdly the Church Property. In lieu of the Church Laws, the same regulations as to doctrine, discipline, &c., were to be valid among members of the Church, *as contract.*

The Church of Ireland in consequence of this great statute became a 'Free Church.' But the expression 'Free Church' has given rise to a popular misapprehension as to the total exemption of voluntary religious societies from the jurisdiction of the ordinary courts of law. Where property and civil rights are at stake, in the last resort, those tribunals to which alone all citizens must perforce submit, will of necessity have to decide between conflicting parties. By the general assent of the members of any religious communion, recourse to the secular courts may be avoided, but in case of dispute waxing warm, general assent is just that element which is wanting. The members of Free Churches, like those of other associations, are bound together by contract, and in case of an alleged and denied *breach of contract*, or in case of a disputed *construction of contract*, who is to decide ! What could appear to be more outside the cognisance of an ordinary court of law than the question whether doctrines preached by the minister of a Free Church are the true doctrines of that church, or more within the province of that church itself to decide than the question who should officiate as minister in its own church ? Yet these are matters which in the last few years the courts of law have had to determine. Property is left on trust to be applied to certain religious purposes specified in the trust deed. It may be that the Thirty-nine Articles are recited, or referred to by the deed. If so the question may arise, are the doctrines preached in conformity with the doctrines of the Thirty-nine Articles ? A few years ago the officiating minister of a congregation of Particular Baptists was dismissed from his chapel and charge by the majority of his congregation, *but* he disputed the lawfulness of the dismissal, and persisted in attempting to enter the chapel, from which he was excluded by force. Thus a point was reached when, whatever may be said about the independence of voluntary churches, it became necessary for a 'mere court of law' to decide who was the true minister of a congregation of Particular Baptists. Each party to the dispute was equally ready to 'appeal to Cæsar;' the minister promptly indicting his opponents before a criminal court for rioting, and the congregation applying for an injunction in Chancery, to restrain their accuser from entering the chapel, *or from acting as their minister*.

The court examined the trust deed, inquired as to whether the action of the congregation was within its provisions, and ultimately decided in favour of the minister. In a civilised country, there can be no freedom from the obligations created by contracts, and that extreme independence which some would claim for religious associations is little better than a dream.

We have seen in an earlier chapter how the construction of the Ecclesiastical Laws of England, and of the articles, doctrines, ordinances, &c., of the Established Church, is the duty of the ecclesiastical courts, and ultimately of the Privy Council. Were these laws, articles, doctrines, &c., made valid by way of contract merely, it is by no means clear that they would be either differently construed or less rigidly enforced. The principles of construction are the same in the Privy Council as in the High Court of Justice; and it is abundantly clear that the authority of the latter could not be excluded. In case of dispute it would be with a Free Church of England as it was with the Particular Baptists, and as it has been with many other Free Churches. A clergyman persists, it may be, upon preaching doctrines, or officiating in a manner, contrary to the provisions of the trust deeds. One of two things must happen; either agreement with the adversary, and that quickly; or a riot at the church door, with 'Cæsar' in the person of the inevitable policeman, or represented by an order of a 'mere court of law.' The importance of the change effected in the position of a church by disconnection with the State, depends of course upon the closeness of the connection that previously existed, and upon the principles adopted in carrying out disendowment. In Ireland the change was very considerable, as the influence of the State exerted through the royal prerogative, through lay patronage, and through parliamentary control, was very great, and disestablishment in that country was necessarily followed by the creation of a new church organisation.

In such a case, on the other hand, as that of the Church of Scotland, with its own organisation complete from the Kirk Session to the General Assembly; without any royal supremacy, for the relationship of the Crown to the Church of Scotland is a purely ornamental one, and with its patronage within its own control, it is difficult to see what serious change in the position of the church would be caused by an Act of mere Disestablishment. It is true that parliamentary control according to constitutional theory is as supreme over the Scotch Establishment as over that of England, or as over that of Ireland before 1869. But most assuredly any attempt on the part of Parliament to exercise such a superintendence over the affairs of the Scotch Church, as it without hindrance exercises over that of England, would raise a protest against 'Erastianism' from the Northern Church such as no Parliament would like to face. As has been pointed out earlier in this work, the formularies, ritual, &c., of the English Church are contained in the Prayer Book, which is incorporated with the Act of Uniformity, a statute which Parliament has several times amended during the present reign. In England there is no other supreme governing authority but Parliament; for Convocation of course cannot be considered in that light, possessing almost no recognised power, and not even containing, like the present disestablished Church of Ireland, and the Church of Scotland, any representation of the lay element in the church. State endowment, on the other hand, is to the Scotch, as to any other church, a matter of great importance, and affects the interests of the nation at large as well as of the church itself.

It is not desirable here to enter upon any controversial topics, further than is necessary to explain our subject; but from what has already been said, readers may be left to judge whether the policy of religious equality as pursued in Ireland can justly be described as a destruction or an abolition of the church whose connection with the State was completely extinguished by the Act of 1869.

The actual and material differences which exist between the status of an 'Established' and a 'Free' Church have been above mentioned, yet it is not intended to suggest that there are not many other considerations of importance, though of a less tangible nature, which may greatly influence the judgment to be formed upon the results arising from the connection of Church and State. By many persons supreme importance is attached to what is called the 'national recognition of religion, and to these such a statute as that of 1869 appears to be nothing less than an Act of National Apostacy. Yet is it not true, as Sir Roundell Palmer, no enemy of Established Churches, in the debate on the second reading of the Irish Church Act, expressed it, that national religion is the religion of the people who constitute the nation? Is it anything different from the sum of the religion of individuals, and is this necessarily less, under a system of voluntaryism than where a 'state' religion prevails? Is Ireland nationally or individually a less religious country at the present day than it was before 1869? The question of Establishment *versus* Voluntaryism must be looked at from both sides, as affecting the nation as a whole, and as affecting the special church under consideration: but before such questions as these can be answered, it would be well to apprehend clearly the main points of distinction between an established and a voluntary system, to elucidate which, without going into too great detail, has been the main object of the present chapter.

It has been said that the National Church offers a 'standard from which to dissent,' and thus its position regulates and steadies, and moderates the action of those under the influence of religious enthusiasts, whose extravagance, as in the United States, would otherwise know no bounds. On the whole, the political system, as it affects religion, must be considered with reference to the existing condition of things. At one age and in one country a State-supported religion may be of the greatest benefit, or be almost essential, to the national welfare, whilst at another age, or in another country, the State connection may do more harm than good. The day is past when constitutions either in State or Church can be regarded abstractedly, as being absolutely perfect, and fit for immediate and universal application upon their own intrinsic merits, without regard to the special necessities of the time, or to their probable practical working.

CHAPTER XI.

THE CHURCH OF SCOTLAND.

IN Scotland the growth and history of the Church were very different from what we have seen in England. The former country owed its early Christianity not to the Roman monks who accompanied Augustin, but to the missionary efforts of St. Columba and St. Kentigern, better known by his Celtic name of St. Mungo. The Celtic Christianity thus spread through the country differed in several respects from the Roman pattern, and it was not till after the lapse of centuries, and the introduction of English influences and customs, caused by the influx of fugitives from the South at the time of the Norman Conquest, that Christianity of the purely Roman type gained the ascendant. Of all the exiles none exercised such influence as Margaret, sister of Edgar Atheling, who, after the expulsion from England of the Saxon line of sovereigns, fled to Scotland, where she became the wife of Malcolm Canmore. To St. Margaret and to her son St. David it was mainly due that a religion of the type established in England prevailed over the old Celtic system of the Culdees. Melrose, Holyrood, Kelso, Dryburgh, Jedburgh, and many other abbeys owed their foundation to King David, as did a large proportion of the Scottish sees. The constitution of Glasgow was copied from Salisbury, that of Dunfermline from Canterbury, that of Melrose from Rievaulx, in Yorkshire. As time went on the ecclesiastics acquired in Scotland, as in England, immense wealth and influence. They wielded great power in the Estates, and often furnished to the Sovereign his chief adviser in the person of a cardinal or archbishop. The bishops in Scotland were not, as in England, a constituent part of *one* House of Parliament only, leaving the other free from their influence. In the Northern kingdom, it may perhaps be necessary to remind English readers, the estates of the realm formed but one assembly, or, as Andrew Fairservice put it, 'in puir auld Scotland's Parliament they a' sat thegither, cheek by jowl, and then they didna need to hae the same blethers twice ower again.'[1] The bishops, moreover, formed a portion of that all-important committee of Parliament called the Lords of the Articles, which in fact absorbed within itself the greater share of Parliamentary authority.

The ecclesiastical courts in Scotland, as in England, had acquired large authority over purely civil matters, their sentences of excommunication, or 'letters of cursing,' to use the common expression, being the favourite process by which the obligations of contract were enforced, a process duly supported by the civil power. In Scotland, certainly not less than in England, had the vices of the ecclesiastics in the age preceding the Reformation excited general indignation and disgust; and thus before attacks upon the Roman Catholic doctrines had

[1] *Rob Roy.*

become formidable, the excessive power and wealth of the ecclesiastics had excited general envy, and their corruption had called forth rebukes from the best of the Churchmen themselves, and from Parliament. Great effect was probably produced in the popular mind by the sharp satires of those play-writers [1] who chose as their favourite theme the vicious life of the religious orders. Thus when the war of doctrine at length burst forth, the Reformers found a powerful ally in the feeling of enmity to the priesthood which was widely spread among the people.

James V. did not die till the year 1542; yet throughout his reign King and Parliament, while inclined to favour reforms, were thoroughly orthodox in their attachment to the doctrines of 'Holy Kirk.' Queen Mary was but a week old at her father's death, and in the first Parliament of the new reign the attention of the Estates was called by the Regent to the fact that there was 'a spreading of heretics, mair and mair, in the realm, sawand damnable opinions contrair to the faith and laws of Haly Kirk' and to the laws of the land. Nevertheless throughout the whole of Mary's reign the Protestant doctrines continued to spread.

[1] The most famous of these was old Sir David Lindsay of the Mount. Readers of *Marmion* may remember the description of the Lord Lyon King at Arms in Canto IV.—

'How in the glances of his eye
A penetrating, keen, and sly
Expression found its home;
The flash of that satiric rage
Which, bursting on the early stage,
Branded the vices of the age
And broke the keys of Rome.'

It would be of course quite impossible in such a work as the present to give even the merest sketch of the history of the Scotch Reformation, but two or three characteristics may be pointed out which strongly distinguish it from the English Reformation, and which have had much to do with the making of the Scottish Church system of the present day. In England the rupture with Rome was created by Henry VIII. His son was an ardent reformer. Elizabeth's throne depended upon her power to resist the Roman Catholic powers of the Continent and the Romanist intrigues of her own subjects. The Reformers in the matter of popular influence followed rather than led the monarchs and their statesmen. Cranmer, in order to please the King, ransacking the universities for precedents and arguments in favour of the divorce of Queen Catharine, was a Church reformer of the English kind. John Knox dictating to Queen Mary at Holyrood, with the sympathies of the Scotch people on his side, was a reformer of a very different kind. The Scotch Reformers were great popular leaders, as well as preachers of a reformed religion. In Scotland during Mary's minority and during her reign the Court was closely connected with the Guises and the French Court, and had at heart the objects of the Catholic League. The Scottish Church had in its early days to struggle hard against Popery, and in later times against prelacy, and these struggles were closely interwoven with the arduous contest of the nation against absolute monarchical power and arbitrary foreign dictation. During the reigns preceding the Revolution of 1688 the Church found strong supporters among all who valued their rights as free citizens, or who as Scotchmen resented the exercise of English control. Hence its national character during these trying times formed a marked contrast with that of the Episcopalian or foreign system which succeeding sovereigns tried so hard to establish north of the Border, and it was at length found that presbyterianism, though subjected to the severest persecution, could not be suppressed. Like the burning bush seen by Moses, which is still the emblem of the Scottish Church, though on fire, it was not consumed.[1]

A few words must be said upon the Scottish Reformation, and the ultimate triumph of a moderate presbyterianism over an episcopalian system.

Before the year 1560 Protestant doctrines must have made great way among the people. Knox had been loudly preaching that the Pope was Antichrist, and that by the law of Heaven the Roman Church had no right to the teinds. Nevertheless in 1558, by the burning of Walter Mill at St. Andrews, the adherents of the old faith showed that they had still the power as well as the will to persecute, and hence, for mutual defence, the Lords of the Congregation, as the leading men among the Protestants were called, bound themselves together by bond or covenant to resist oppression. They and Knox determined freely to practise their religion by the regular reading in all the parishes on Sundays of the Book of Common Prayer (*i.e.* Edward's Prayer-Book), and to petition the Sovereign to establish the Protestant religion.

In consequence of the reliance of the Queen Regent on

[1] The well-known emblem of the Scotch Church is the 'Burning Bush,' with the motto, 'Nec tamen consumebatur.'

a French army, and the despatch of English troops by Elizabeth to assist the Lords of the Congregation, an entirely new direction was given to public feeling in Scotland, where hitherto the strongest sentiment of the nation had been hostility to their 'auld enemies of England.' In the year 1560 the Queen Regent died, and Queen Mary returned to Scotland, to find on her arrival that Parliament had accepted the Protestant confession of faith, had suppressed the mass, and had in fact given full effect to the petition of Knox and the Lords of the Congregation. Seven years later, after Mary had ceased to reign, these statutes, which hitherto had been without the Royal assent,[1] were confirmed by the Estates under the regency of Murray. After the death of Knox and throughout the reign of James VI. the contest between Presbytery and Prelacy inclined sometimes to the one side and sometimes to the other. The early Scotch Reformers, and Knox among them, had regarded Popery rather than Prelacy as the enemy of the Reformation, and had seen the importance of maintaining terms of friendship and alliance with the Reformed Church of England.

The Reformers had had among them a large proportion of the influential classes, but times underwent a change and many of the nobles and landowners, who had been ready enough to give assent to the Protestant Confession of Faith, began to look with a much more doubtful eye on the provisions of the Books of Discipline; particularly as they affected the utilisation of the old ecclesiastical revenues for Knox's three great objects, the support of the ministry,

[1] It is not clear that in Scotland the Royal assent was essential to the validity of Acts of the Estates.

the education of the people, and the relief of the poor. The Church had early organised itself into a gradation of Church courts, much like the system of the present day; but Parliament forbore for many years to suppress entirely the Episcopal hierarchy which had previously prevailed. Hence arose a curious combination of systems. Though archbishops and bishops were recognised, their authority was limited and they were made subject to the courts of the Church and to the General Assembly. The territorial classes favoured the Episcopate for reasons which did them little credit; and the Scotch public appears to have been fully alive to the motives at work. If the immense estates belonging to the unreformed Church were to be utilised for the benefit of the Reformers and the nation as contemplated by Knox, the large number of landowners who had already benefited by an absorption of Church property would have to part with their recently acquired wealth. It was the aim, therefore, of a considerable part of the aristocracy to maintain Episcopal dignitaries without allowing them to receive more than a small proportion of the revenues of the sees. The revenues would in this way not be dispersed, and arrangements could be made with each bishop on appointment by which, in return for a small stipend, a large share might be retained by the lay owner of what was formerly Church property. In short, many of the nobility favoured the Episcopal system, but wished to leave to the bishop as small a portion as was possible of the old endowments.

The Church, however, whenever it could find an opportunity of freely avowing its sympathies, declared steadily against prelacy. The very names of archbishop and bishop, dean, chancellor, and chapter seemed to be 'slanderous and offensive, to the ears of many of the brethren appearing to sound of Papistry.'[1]

The mind of James vacillated. In the year 1592, after his marriage with a princess of Denmark, he inclined towards Presbytery. The Parliament repealed the 'Black Acts' of eight years earlier which had authorised Episcopacy, and once more re-established the Presbyterian polity. But James, supported by a nobility still hungering after the wealth of the Church, turned later in his reign again towards Episcopacy; an inclination which his removal to England tended to strengthen. The Divine-right Bishop of the Court of St. James naturally proved a more agreeable courtier than the Scottish Reformer standing up boldly for the subjects' right of resistance to a sovereign who should 'exceed his bounds.' The King, who a short time before had declared the English service to be 'but an ill-said mass,' now became devotedly attached to the English polity and ritual. Scotch ecclesiastics came to London to receive at the hands of English bishops, and in the authorised fashion, the true apostolical succession. In their own country the term applied to these mock bishops, viz. tulchans, showed the popular appreciation of motives which undoubtedly brought many powerful allies to support the Episcopal system.[2] Efforts were also made to force upon the Scotch certain practices of English ritual and religious observance. They were to take the communion on their knees, and were to observe Christmas

---

[1] General Assembly at Perth, 1572.

[2] The tulchan was the stuffed calf, employed in milking, to induce the cow readily to yield her milk. Here the bishop was the tulchan; the Church was the cow, milked of her revenues for the benefit of the nobility.

and some other days as religious festivals. James would have gone still further in this direction had he listened to the advice given even then by Laud to make 'that stubborn Kirk stoop still more to the English pattern.'

But James was wiser than his son, and dared not 'play fast and loose with his word.' He perceived clearly, as he tells us himself, that Laud 'knew not the stomach of that people; but he himself called to mind the story of his grandmother the Queen Regent, who having been inveigled into breaking her promise, never again saw good-day, but from thence, being much beloved before, was despised by her people.'

Thus the attempt to set up Episcopacy under James was associated with the most sordid motives.[1] Charles pursued the same ends, but with greater steadfastness of purpose. Not only was he determined to have bishops; he intended them to exercise real episcopal power, and to enjoy the old ecclesiastical revenues, a policy which once more drove the territorial classes into hostility to the Episcopalian system. But the efforts of Charles under the guidance of Laud were not confined to setting up Episcopal organisation and authority, and recovering for the bishops the Episcopal revenues. Laud and the newly created Scottish bishops revised the English Prayer-Book, introducing a few changes in the Romanist direction, and drew up a Book of Canons for the government of the Scottish Church and clergy, and the King in right of his alleged prerogative ordered general obedience

---

[1] The motives operating towards the setting up of Episcopacy in Scotland are very forcibly pointed out in the Duke of Argyll's *Presbytery Examined*.

and uniformity to both Service Book and Canons. The history of the riot in St. Giles's, caused by the attempt of the surpliced Dean of Edinburgh to read the new liturgy on the famous Sunday of July 1637, is known to all. The liturgy was rightly credited to Laud, and Laud himself was popularly credited with the intention of restoring Popery. The worshippers at St. Giles's thought it was the mass itself which they heard sounding in their ears. Protestant enthusiasm spread through the country. The following year the National Covenant was after religious services enthusiastically renewed in the Greyfriars churchyard in Edinburgh and subscribed by multitudes throughout Scotland. 'Noblemen, barons, gentlemen, burgesses, ministers, and commons' took a solemn oath to maintain the Protestant religion, and to stand by and defend the King and the laws, and pronounced their abhorrence of Papistry and their detestation of the Roman Antichrist.

The party of the Covenanters, which soon comprised nearly the whole of Presbyterian Scotland, was not satisfied with demanding the withdrawal of the Service Book and Canons; they asked also for a free Assembly and a free Parliament. The General Assembly met in the Cathedral Church of Glasgow, in November 1638, with the sanction of the King and in the presence of his Commissioner, but business had hardly begun before it became clear that the views of the Sovereign and of the Assembly were irreconcilable. The latter was determined to put the bishops upon their trial, and entirely to subject them to the assemblies of the Church. The former not only opposed these demands, but refused to allow the presence of elders or laymen in Church councils. A crisis had now come. The Royal Commissioner withdrew from the Assembly and dissolved it in the King's name. But the Assembly, among whom were no fewer than seventeen peers, and many of the most influential men, lay and clerical, in Scotland, refusing to disperse, at once re-established the Presbyterian polity, abolished all the Acts of the late packed Assemblies of King James, and condemned the Service Book and Canons.

These proceedings of the great General Assembly of Glasgow were ratified the following year by the Estates.

When the war broke out between the King and the Parliament of England, the Puritan party saw the necessity of gaining as an ally the powerful army of Scotland. Hence the Presbyterians and the Puritans began to draw closer together, but it was not till after the Covenant, now become the 'Solemn League and Covenant,' had been accepted by the English Parliament, as an international agreement binding on the three kingdoms, that the Scottish army was put in motion. Popery and prelacy were to be extirpated, if necessary, by force, and religion was to be reformed after the pattern of the best Reformed Churches.

The religious contest was now shifted from Scotland to the meeting of the Assembly of Divines in the Jerusalem Chamber at Westminster. Here, after long debate and careful examination, the main standards of the Scotch Church were decided upon—the Confession of Faith, and the Larger and Shorter Catechisms. These were intended as the final settlement of Presbyterian doctrine, not merely for Scotland, but for England and Ireland also, throughout which countries there was to be but one Church.

The Westminster Assembly had, of course, no direct authority to prescribe doctrine to the Scotch people. Indeed, the Scotch Commissioners had not even a place within that Assembly. The three 'standards'[1] above mentioned, which form the religious basis of the National Church and of the other Presbyterian Churches of Scotland to this day, owed their authority to the General Assemblies of the Scotch Church of the years 1647 and 1648, by which they were examined and approved, the Estates subsequently ratifying the Acts of the Assemblies. Hopeful as at this time appeared to be the prospects of Presbytery, it was not long before it was seen that that system had no chance of becoming predominant in England; whilst in Scotland very shortly afterwards Cromwell used his soldiers to disperse the General Assembly, as he had used them to disperse the Parliament of England. Though deprived of its General Assembly, the Church in other respects enjoyed a fair amount of liberty during the Protectorate, and on the restoration of Charles II. Churchmen confidently anticipated that the Presbyterian polity would be re-established in all its completeness. To bring this about the Church sent Commissioners to London. But the King bore no love to Presbytery, and Sharpe, one of the Commissioners, after a short stay in London, returned, not for the purpose of establishing the Church on a Presbyterian basis, but to spend the remainder of his days as the primate of its hated rival—

---

[1] The Confessions of Faith and the Catechisms are but 'subordinate standards' of the Presbyterian Churches, the Holy Scriptures themselves constituting the true standard, and containing the 'only rule of faith and manners.'

namely, as Archbishop of St. Andrews. The first Parliament of the Restoration repealed by one sweeping enactment all the Acts passed since 1640, including those in favour of the Presbyterian system. Scotch ecclesiastics once more journeyed to London to receive fresh inspiration in the orthodox fashion from the imposition of English Episcopal hands, and to renew in their own country the stream which, for the second time, had almost run dry. From the Restoration to the Revolution of 1688 the attempts of the Crown never slackened to thrust upon the Scotch people the obnoxious prelatic system of England, with the natural result of making prelacy the more odious to the nation, from the persecution with which it was accompanied.

In the present day few enlightened Presbyterians think that Episcopalian church government is necessarily associated with civil tyranny in the State, but it undoubtedly happened in Scotland that from incidental causes the triumph of prelacy was throughout closely connected with the cause of absolute monarchy, or with the selfish objects of a greedy aristocracy. None who read the history of Scotland during the sixteenth and seventeenth centuries can wonder that in that country Episcopacy acquired a bad name. In the first half of the eighteenth century such importance as that religious system still retained was due more to its political connection with Jacobitism than to its ecclesiastical character, and when the Hanoverian line of monarchs had become firmly established Scotch Episcopalianism rapidly ceased to be an element of any weight in either the civil or religious life of the nation.

The statutes passed in Scotland after the Revolution are to the Scottish Church what the statutes passed in England after the Restoration are to the English Church. We have seen how the legal position of the Church of England was defined and its Prayer Book authorised by Charles II.'s Act of Uniformity. By a statute of William and Mary the Westminster Confession of Faith having been read to the Estates, was ratified and confirmed, all previous Acts against Popery and Papists were revived, and Presbyterian Church government and discipline were established—'that is to say, the government of the Church by Kirk Sessions, Presbyteries, Provincial Synods, and General Assemblies.'[1] This was giving legal effect to the Church's Claim of Right, in which it was declared that 'prelacy and the superiority of any office in the Church above presbyters is, and hath been, a great and insupportable grievance and trouble to this nation, and contrary to the inclinations of the generality of the people ever since the Reformation;' a claim which had been to some extent already given effect to by the Act of the previous session abolishing prelacy. In 1693 the Confession of Faith was made obligatory upon all ministers of the Church, and a few years later, when the dread of the effect of a union with a prelatic kingdom upon religious orthodoxy was affecting the minds of most Scotchmen, it was imposed in addition upon all professors in the Universities and teachers in schools. It is narrated that not merely the Confession of Faith, but also the other Westminster standards were to have been brought before the Scotch Parliament; but that

[1] Act 1690, c. 5.

the House, after hearing the first, 'grew restive and impatient, and could stand out no longer,' and it is certain that the Parliamentary minutes record an agreement to leave out of the Act all mention of the Larger and the Shorter Catechism.

The Covenant was not renewed; on the contrary, it was entirely ignored, to the intense disgust of the extremer section of Presbyterians, who would not listen for a moment to the suggestion 'that the inclinations of the generality of the people' should be consulted when the question seemed to them to be one of obedience or of disobedience to the decrees of Heaven. The Covenanter of the old type rejected the notion that 'vox populi' was necessarily, or even probably, 'vox Dei.' He himself knew, without a shade of doubt crossing his mind, what was the will of God; and he had seen himself, and had found in the Scriptures, many instances of the people being in flagrant opposition to the injunctions of the Most High.

Owing, however, in great measure to the wisdom of William III., the form of religion established was a moderate Presbyterianism. The Confession of Faith was the sole *statutory* doctrinal standard of religion in Scotland; yet, in fact, the basis of the general religious instruction given in that country to ninety-nine out of every hundred Presbyterian children has been and is, not the Confession of Faith, but the Shorter Catechism. In short, as far as the masses of the people are concerned, the Shorter Catechism, taught in all the Presbyterian schools, constitutes the true religious creed of Scotland.

William was desirous of making the Scotch Establishment more widely comprehensive of the various existing forms of Protestantism than the Church was willing to allow; and it was some time before he understood the full meaning of the Church's claim to independence, and of its vigorous repudiation of 'the headship' of any earthly sovereign. The King endeavoured to force upon the Church courts, and upon the General Assembly itself, Episcopalian clergymen who accepted the Confession of Faith and were loyal to the new Constitution. But that the King or the civil authority should prescribe who were to be members of the General Assembly was accounted the rankest Erastianism, the boldest invasion of the rights of the Church, and so strained in consequence did the relations become between Church and King that the Royal Commissioner actually dissolved the Assembly without appointing a day for its reassembling. It was two years before it met again on the summons of the Crown; and then it was only by timely concession from the King that a rupture was avoided and the crisis passed. From that time to the present the General Assembly has been annually held, and the Crown and the Church have continued on amicable terms. But the existing practice of adjournment invented by the Royal Commissioner and the Moderator of the first General Assembly after the Revolution, still bears witness to the claim of 'supremacy' made by both Church and King. At whose summons should the Church assemble, at the King's or at its own? Every year, when the General Assembly has completed its business, a day is appointed for its meeting the year following, by the Royal Commissioner 'in the name of the Queen' and by the Moderator 'in the name of the Lord Jesus Christ.' And as Commissioner and Moderator have agreed to select the same day, no awkward question arises.

When the union between the two kingdoms was in contemplation, the Scotch were naturally afraid that their established religion might suffer in consequence of their representatives being outnumbered by those of England in the Parliament of Great Britain, and that it would be in the power of future Parliaments to set aside the Revolution Settlement of the Church. Hence they endeavoured to accomplish an impossibility, viz. to bind their posterity for ever. By the 'Act of Security' of 1705 the intention of the Scotch Parliament was to secure 'unalterably the true Protestant religion as then professed within the kingdom,' and it was therefore enacted that the said religion, and 'the worship, discipline, and government of this Church, should continue without any alteration to the people of this land in all succeeding generations.' Future sovereigns of Great Britain on their accession were to swear to maintain the said settlement of religion, and the whole Act of Security was to be a 'fundamental and essential condition of any treaty or union to be concluded between the two kingdoms, without any alteration thereof, or derogation thereto, in any sort, for ever.' In 1707 these provisions were incorporated in the English and Scotch Acts ratifying the Union, each of which declared that the above-quoted Act of Security, along with the Articles of Union, should 'be and continue in *all time coming* the sure and perpetual foundation of a complete and entire union of the two kingdoms.'[1]

[1] Notwithstanding all these precautions, the Act of Security has been amended, and partially repealed by a statute of the present reign dealing with the religious tests which the former Act strictly imposed upon the office-bearers of the Scotch Universities.

CHAPTER XII.

THE CHURCH OF SCOTLAND (*continued*).

The Presbyterian form of government finally established by the Revolution settlement remains substantially unchanged to the present day. The basis of the whole system is the Kirk Session of the Parish, in which the minister presides as moderator, and in which two or more elders selected from the male communicants, who are also heads of families, have seats. By various Acts of Assembly it has been made incumbent on elders to accept the Confession of Faith, though by the statute law no test of orthodoxy is imposed upon the lay members of any of the Church Courts. The Court next in order above the Kirk Session is the Presbytery, which comprises all the parishes within its bounds. The members of the Presbytery are the parish ministers and elders, or rather the minister and one elder from each parish. If there is a University within the bounds of the Presbytery, the Professors of Divinity (if they are ministers) also have seats. The bounds of Presbyteries as well as their number have been fixed by the General Assembly. Presbyteries vary greatly in size. That of Edinburgh, for instance, comprises between forty and fifty parishes, and that of Glasgow more than seventy parishes, while in thinly populated districts a Presbytery contains, perhaps, only half a dozen parishes. At the present time the Presbyteries number eighty-four. Next above the Presbyteries are the **Provincial Synods**, of which there are sixteen, each comprising within its bounds a certain number of Presbyteries. The members of each Synod are the members of the Presbyteries within it.

Above the Synods is the General Assembly, at once the Supreme Legislature of the Church and the Supreme Court of Appeal in all ecclesiastical causes. This, the governing body of the Church, is constituted out of representatives of both clergy and laity. Each Presbytery sends two or more ministers and one or more 'ruling elders' to the Assembly; each of the Royal Burghs sends an elder; and each of the Universities sends, as it chooses, either a minister or an elder. In the present day the Churches of India in connection with the Church of Scotland also have representatives in the Assembly. By the statute of 1690 referred to in the last chapter it was stipulated that the General Assembly should be allowed to meet periodically, and should be composed of ministers and elders in the manner it should appoint in accordance with 'the custom and practice of Presbyterian government throughout the whole kingdom;' that it should have power to censure erring ministers, to redress all Church disorders, and to deprive any minister, whom it might convict or find contumacious, of stipend and benefice. The constitution of the General Assembly and its system of legislating have been framed by its own 'Acts of Assembly.' One of these, known as the Barrier Act of 1697, in the main regulates the procedure to be followed in legislating for the Church; its object being, by requiring the reference of 'overtures' —that is, proposals accepted by the General Assembly—to the Presbyteries for report to the General Assembly of the year following, to ensure that measures should not pass into law till the general opinion of the Church in their favour has been obtained. But, as this would cause considerable delay, it is a common practice for the Assembly to pass 'interim Acts,' which become valid at once, and so remain unless they are rejected by the Assembly of the year following for not having obtained the general support of the Church. The Assembly meets every year in Edinburgh in the month of May, and its business is conducted in the presence of a Lord High Commissioner representing the Crown, who is usually a Peer connected with Scotland, but not necessarily or usually a member of the Church. His functions are of a purely ornamental kind. When the General Assembly is not in session business is conducted by the Commission of Assembly, which meets at fixed periods, or if desirable upon the mere summons of the Moderator.

Whilst the Church repudiates all inequalities of rank among ministers, there is thus a regular gradation of Church Courts from Kirk Session to General Assembly. The judicial authority of these Courts consists in their power to inflict spiritual censures upon members of the Church and to depose offending ministers, who thereby become at once deprived of their parochial emoluments. The minister, however, cannot be made amenable to a lower court than the Presbytery; for, as we have seen, he is himself moderator of the Kirk Session, and when he is absent from it no business can be transacted. From Kirk

Session to Presbytery, from Presbytery to Synod, from Synod to General Assembly an appeal lies; and this is not merely at the instance of a dissatisfied party, for the superior court has jurisdiction to bring before itself for review the decisions of an inferior tribunal. So long as the decisions of these Church Courts are given in the lawful exercise of their judicial powers, and in matters purely ecclesiastical, they are not subject to the review of any civil court whatever. No appeal lies from the General Assembly to the Court of Session, to the House of Lords, or to the Crown. But should the Church Courts overstep their limits and abuse their powers, the Court of Session will give redress to an injured party against what *it considers* [1] the illegal sentence of an ecclesiastical court.

In many respects the authority which a Presbytery exercises over the parishes within it is analogous to the authority of a Bishop over his diocese. In case of breach or neglect of duty by a minister, or of his being the subject of public scandal or suspected of heretical doctrine, it is to the Presbytery in the first instance that he must render account; whilst in the purely ecclesiastical function of ordination to the ministry the Presbytery in Scotland corresponds to the Bishop in England. It is the Presbytery which, after due examination into the morals, orthodoxy, and learning of a candidate, licenses him to preach the Gospel, and the licensee, then known as a probationer, though incapable of administering the Sacraments of the Church, is in most other respects

---

[1] The real power resides in that authority which defines for practical purposes the limits of the rival tribunals.

qualified to exercise the ordinary ministerial functions. The probationer, after a period of trial, must once more establish his fitness before a Presbytery, must declare his assent to the Scriptures as containing the only rule of faith and manners, his acceptance of the Confession of Faith, and his determination to maintain the Presbyterian form of Church government. The power to administer the Sacraments, the complete authority of a true minister of the Church, is bestowed, as in England, by the imposition of hands, the hands of the Presbytery in Scotland transmitting to the new minister much the same species of spiritual authority which in England can only be communicated by the hands of the Bishop. The ceremony of ordination takes place when the new minister for the first time enters upon the charge of a parish.

Besides the extensive judicial powers possessed by the Church Courts, legislative authority of a wide though rather indefinite kind also belongs to them. In the present day their authority, whether judicial or legislative, is at all events limited to members of the Church. But this was by no means the view that the Church itself took in the earlier part of last century, when the Presbytery of Edinburgh discharged from his clerical functions an Episcopalian clergyman for using the English ritual, which had been abandoned by the Scotch Episcopalians and by the Bishops themselves for the greater part of a century. The clergyman who disputed the authority of the Presbytery was sent to prison, and the Court of Session fully supported the legality of the action of the Church. The House of Lords, however, reversed the decision of the Court of Session, and a Toleration Act,

XII.] AUTHORITY OF THE GENERAL ASSEMBLY. 161

subsequently passed, put such stretches of authority for ever beyond the reach of ecclesiastical intolerance.

The much-vexed question of the independence of the Church cannot be adequately discussed here. It is easy to lay down general principles, very difficult to apply them in particular cases. 'The General Assembly,' it is said, 'may define or explain articles of faith, condemn heretical opinions, and make canons for the better establishment of the government and discipline of the Church, provided its resolutions be consistent with the laws of the realm from which the National Church derives its whole authority.'[1] Again, the courts of law have decided that the General Assembly has no power to pass Acts affecting civil rights and patrimonial interests, or to alter the law of the land, and in such cases the Court of Session will give relief. The question of the legal validity of an Act of Assembly enabling a congregation to veto the appointment of a presentee whose patron had a right by the statute law to present, raised for the consideration of the Scotch Courts and the House of Lords the whole relationship between Church and State in Scotland. The decisions of the Courts, limiting the 'independence' claimed by the Church as one of its fundamental principles, caused the disruption of 1843. These decisions have nevertheless made it clear that absolute independence cannot exist in a National Church—that is to say, in a Church which belongs to the nation. Where there is a State Church, the Church and its officers hold certain definite positions recognised by the law of the land, and it is vain to expect the State entirely to forego its authority in

[1] Erskine's *Institutes of the Law of Scotland*.

M

matters which so intimately affect its own interests. 'When two authorities are up' confusion can only be avoided by the one or the other eventually becoming 'supreme.' The contest in Scotland ended in the legal victory of the State over the ecclesiastical authority of the Established Church. An Act of Assembly is in law waste paper, if it is in conflict with an Act of Parliament, and the law laid down by the Court of Session is, until overruled, as much entitled to obedience as an Act of Parliament. The history of the dispute between Church and State, which ended in the Disruption and the rise of the Free Church, conclusively proves that an Established Church is necessarily subordinate to the State if differences arise between them.

A similar conflict is seen at the present day in England, though there the contest lies not between civil and religious legislatures and tribunals, representing State and Church, as it did in Scotland, but rather between the only legislature and tribunals which exist, on the one hand, and the claim of the individual clergyman to be a law unto himself on the other. Whilst, however, the Church of Scotland can no longer successfully maintain its absolute independence, enough has been said to show how much greater *in fact* is its power of legislating and adjudicating on its own affairs than that possessed by the sister Church in England. Parliamentary interference with the affairs of the Church of Scotland, if carried any length, would raise an outcry against Erastianism amply sufficient to bring such interference to an end, or, if it continued, to cause a fresh disruption, and even the downfall of the Church. If attention is paid rather to what exists in practice than to mere constitutional theory, that which will most strike an impartial inquirer is the *slightness* of the hold of State over Church in Scotland, and how small *virtually* is the difference of position in that country between an 'Established' and a 'Free Church' in everything not connected with the subject of endowment.

If the control of State over State Church is in Scotland very slight, it would be a mistake on the other hand to suppose that the non-established churches enjoy absolute freedom. The Free Church, for instance, there is strong reason to believe, is absolutely tied down to its standards, so that a majority of its General Assembly, however large, cannot legislate so as to modify them. The Free Church, as is well known, was in 1843 strongly opposed to the voluntary principle. The United Presbyterians are pure voluntaries. A projected union of the Free with the United Presbyterian Church a few years ago was decried by a section of the former as a defection from the principles of 1843. Had this project been persevered with it may be that a division would have taken place in the former Church. And if so civil interests and a large amount of property would have been involved in a dispute which only the courts of law could have settled. The opinion of very eminent counsel was taken, with the result of its being ascertained that in point of law the Free Church General Assembly, instead of being 'independent,' is strictly limited by the principles of 1843.[1]

[1] See speech by Dr. Begg at Inverness, March 24, 1882 Anyone who takes an interest in the legal status of Churches, Established and Free, considered in relation to their creeds, should

A Royal Commission appointed in the year 1834 to inquire into the condition of religious instruction in Scotland collected a vast mass of information. In the opinion of the Commissioners no institution that ever existed had at so little cost accomplished so much good as the Church of Scotland. And at the present day though there is much dissatisfaction expressed with the existing position of the Church, it stands free from those reproaches which have often been truly made against other State Churches. The sale and purchase of livings, though legal till 1874, was rarely practised in Scotland, public sentiment, the feeling of patrons and ministers, and the limited nature of the right of patronage possessed by the patrons, all combining to render such a traffic generally impossible. 'Fat livings' have no existence in the North. There are no spiritual lords of Parliament, with their incomes of many thousands per annum, to render more glaring the inequality between the lot of fortunate and unfortunate followers of the sacred calling. On the contrary, the Church of Scotland, democratic or republican in constitution, has preserved not merely an equality of rank among its ministers, but also a very general uniformity of moderation in the scale of their remuneration. In creed, in forms of service, in system of government, the Church has been such as the Presbyterians of Scotland of all denominations have always approved and still approve. Though Dissent now prevails to a very large extent, the dissatisfaction of Dissenters with the Church

read Mr. Taylor Innes's *Law of Creeds in Scotland*. There, and in Lord Cockburn's Journal, will be found a discussion of many problems the interest of which is by no means limited to Scotland.

has not been due to any differences upon such matters as these, and the voluntary Churches that have arisen hold precisely the same creeds, pursue precisely the same forms of public worship, and are governed upon precisely the same system as the National Church. As the late Dean of Westminster said of the Presbyterian Churches to an Edinburgh audience,[1] 'theirs is a uniformity which Rome might have enjoined and which Lambeth might envy.' Those who have left the Church have on the whole been more rigidly orthodox than those who have stayed behind. They have gone out not in search of greater freedom for themselves, but because they could no longer remain in a Church tainted with the Erastian character and the religious laxity inseparable from a State connection. In the last and greatest of the secessions, that of 1843, the Free Church in the very act of seceding did, it is true, strongly assert the principle of a National Establishment. But it was a claim of a kind to which in the present day it is impossible for the State to yield; for the alliance contemplated between Church and State was to involve in all matters affecting the national religion an 'independence' on the part of the former authority which left nothing but absolute subservience to the latter.

It is not necessary to give any account of the various secessions from the National Church, or to describe the position which the voluntary Churches have attained, but it is important to recognise the existing state of things, viz. that the religious welfare of the people of Scotland is now-a-days to a very large extent cared for by voluntary

---

[1] Lecture on Church of Scotland to Edinburgh Philosophical Institution.

religious societies, which find in the zeal of their members and in the freewill offerings of their friends ample resources for carrying out the work once supposed to be dependent upon State aid. The National Church, great as are the benefits which it has brought to the nation, is in fact but one among several Churches which go far to rival it in numbers, in wealth, in activity, and in usefulness. Hence the weakness of its position, not as 'a Church,' but as claiming a position which by force of circumstances and through no fault of its own has become an exceptional one.

The resources of the Church of Scotland and the number of its members may be roughly estimated.

The wealth of the Church, due to its connection with the State, consists of teinds, of receipts from burgh funds in some town parishes, of churches,[1] of manses and glebes, and of grants from the Consolidated Fund. The parishes are nearly one thousand in number,[2] and estimating the value of the manses and glebes at 50,000*l.*, the whole provision out of State funds made for the clergy may be taken at between 320,000*l.* and 350,000*l.* per annum, the great bulk of which is supplied by the teinds. In this revenue is included the sum of 16,000*l.* paid annually out of the Exchequer under certain Acts of Parliament authorising the augmentation of small stipends. The only other sums provided by the nation are the annual

---

[1] Churches and manses are maintained in repair out of money raised by assessments upon the heritors. If the manse is in a very dilapidated condition, the heritors may be compelled to erect a new building.

[2] If 'Quoad Sacra' parishes be reckoned the number of parishes would be much larger.

grants of 2,000*l.* to the Royal Commissioner, of 2,000*l.* to the General Assembly to provide 'itinerating preachers,' and of 1,000*l.* to pay certain incidental expenses connected with the annual meeting of the General Assembly.

In Scotland as in England the Established Church draws very largely from voluntary sources. The number of churches belonging to the Scottish Establishment exceeds fifteen hundred, and, as those depending in any degree upon State aid are about one thousand, the remaining five hundred must rely on voluntary support. Since 1845 the Church claims to have created more than three hundred new parishes, many of them with manses and with an average stipend of 120*l.* per annum, provided entirely by the freewill offerings of its friends. The total sums voluntarily raised for all purposes, including increase of stipends, church building and extension endowment of new parishes, home and foreign mission work, and the like, amount, roughly speaking, to about the same figure as those provided by the State. Thus, without pretending to give absolutely accurate statistics, there is reason to believe that the whole income of the National Church may be put roughly at something under, but approaching to, 700,000*l.* per annum, of which one half is provided by the State and the other half out of the present and past liberality of Churchmen.[1] Putting the average annual income of the Free Church as low as 500,000*l.*, and of the United Presbyterians at 350,000*l.*,

---

[1] The late Mr. Baird settled 500,000*l.* on the National Church to meet the spiritual destitution of the people. It is to be expended in promoting sound religious and constitutional principles, based upon Holy Scripture as interpreted by the standards of the Church of Scotland.

the whole coming of course entirely from voluntary sources, it becomes evident how small is the proportion of assistance provided by the State for the maintenance of religion in Scotland.[1]

As regards the number of members of the National Church, it is impossible to make any safe estimate, for no official census has been taken since 1851. On one Sunday in that year, out of 944,000 attendances at church, the Church of Scotland had 351,000, the Free Church 292,000, and the United Presbyterians 159,000.

The recent returns furnished to the newspapers by unofficial persons as to church attendance have been much questioned, and could hardly be taken as a proper basis of calculation. In the last few years, however, Parliamentary returns have been obtained of the number of persons entitled to take part in the election of ministers on the occurring of a vacancy, a system which in 1874 was substituted for patronage. The electors in each parish are the communicants and adherents.[2] In 1874 the communicants numbered 460,000. In 1878 they numbered 515,000. These figures have been much criticised. On the one hand it is said they are too small, as in many cases only showing the numbers that actually communicated in one

---

[1] At the last meeting of the Free Church General Assembly the receipts for the preceding year from all sources and for all purposes amounted to nearly 600,000*l*. During the same year the United Presbyterians raised nearly 400,000*l*.

[2] The electorate is such as would rejoice Mr. Jacob Bright, ladies forming a majority of the electors in every parish in Scotland. *Men of full age* are in a very decided minority, owing to the number of women and children among the communicants. *Adherents* must be of full age.

year, instead of the whole number on the Communion roll. On the other hand it is maintained that they are far too large, the rolls, through carelessness, not having been properly 'purged' in cases of death or other disqualification.¹ The complete accuracy of these returns is of no great importance. There is no doubt that the National Church has a large following and an able and hard-working ministry, and just as little doubt that outside its limits is to be found much of the energetic Presbyterianism of the country. It has been shown conclusively that Scotch Presbyterianism can work and thrive and grow rich without receiving the slightest aid from national funds. The future position of the State Church depends upon the practical wants of the people of Scotland and upon the spread among them of voluntary principles and the desire for religious equality. Upon such broad considerations rather than upon the rivalry of different sects will the future religious system of that country be ultimately settled.

Whether an Established Church be a 'scriptural' or 'unscriptural' institution is not a question about which those who care to dispute are ever likely to agree, and it is certainly not one which need be discussed here. Again, the value of a 'State recognition of religion' is considered a matter of the highest importance; by many persons of much more importance than the mere right of the ministry to endowments out of State funds; but of what, in fact, this recognition consists beyond the presence of the

---

[2] See article by Principal Rainy in the March number of the *Contemporary Review* of 1882.

Royal Commissioner in the General Assembly it is very difficult to ascertain. At all events the object of the present chapter has been simply to deal with the facts of the case, and not to speculate either upon the interpretation of Scripture or upon remote consequences.

Endowment is something tangible and intelligible to all. The word '*Establishment*,' on the contrary, appears to convey very different ideas to the minds of different people, exciting among many Dissenters an exaggerated hostility to a Church singularly like their own, and among many Churchmen an apparent belief that the religion of the nation depends upon the connection being preserved between Church and State. It may be safely predicted that the religious interests of Scotland will depend in the future, as indeed they do mainly at present, not upon any State connection or recognition, whatever it may amount to, but upon the efforts made by the Presbyterian Churches out of their own resources, voluntarily raised, to minister to the religious wants of the Scottish nation.

www.ingramcontent.com/pod-product-compliance
Lightning Source LLC
Chambersburg PA
CBHW032156160426
43197CB00008B/934